ADVANCE PRAISE

"*Mastering Market Entry: USA provides European companies and investors with proven American market-entry mastery. Manny Schoenhuber has written a playbook for European business leaders to follow, showing them how to go about setting up their business to break into the US without making a cultural misstep. 5 stars.*"

—ERIN MCKELVEY, PRESIDENT & CEO OF EUROPEAN
AMERICAN CHAMBER OF COMMERCE TEXAS

"*In Mastering Market Entry: USA, Manny Schoenhuber hails the European mid-market businessperson as a "hidden champion"—someone who has what it takes to succeed, but who hasn't yet embarked upon the process of entering the US market. This guidebook to transacting Transatlantic business is a critically important resource for every European company and can enable your company's success stateside—don't overlook it!*"

—MATTHIAS HOFFMANN, PRESIDENT &
CEO OF GERMAN AMERICAN CHAMBER OF
COMMERCE OF THE SOUTHERN US, INC.

"European companies often consider taking their operations into the US, but the up-front costs make them hesitant to make a commitment. Hesitation, we all know, is a recipe for business failure. Mastering Market Entry: USA should make you bold again. You see, now, how the US is an ideal market for you. International expansion will help hedge you against business risk. Thanks to Manny Schoenhuber's guidance, you should eagerly anticipate significant growth."

—MORTEN SIEM LYNGE, CONSUL GENERAL & HEAD OF ENERGY OF NORTH AMERICA CONSULATE GENERAL OF DENMARK—HOUSTON

"In Mastering Market Entry: USA, Manny Schoenhuber emphasizes to European businesses the significance of acquiring skills in team building, delegation, and collaborative approaches when contemplating business expansion. His guidance, in clear language and based on many years of experience, empowers European companies to establish a business strategy that hinges on effective teamwork, rather than attempting to handle everything independently. By following his advice, you can enter the US market with confidence, positioning your business for success."

—BAUKJE BEE KOTHUIS, CHIEF REPRESENTATIVE OF NETHERLANDS BUSINESS SUPPORT OFFICE IN TEXAS

"Mastering Market Entry: USA encourages European companies to establish a foothold in the thriving US marketplace. Manny Schoenhuber, drawing on his dual identity as an American lawyer with a European background, provides valuable insights into the opportunities awaiting European business people in the US market. His multidimensional background enables him to navigate cultural challenges and understand diverse market dynamics. Readers can benefit significantly from Manny's extensive legal expertise and sound advice."

—AHMET YAVUZHAN ERDEM, COMMERCIAL ATTACHÉ CONSULATE GENERAL OF THE REPUBLIC OF TÜRKIYE IN HOUSTON

"Many European companies spend decades establishing their operations in Europe. They receive much advice on how to expand their business, especially into the US. However, most of the resources do not come from a place of Transatlantic authority. That's where Manny excels. You can trust his advice, as he is having roots in Europe but is experienced at representing successful, European-run businesses in America. Take his methods and ideas for market entry to heart and develop a viable working plan for US expansion."

—ZUZANNA KOBRZYNSKI, HEAD OF FOREIGN TRADE OFFICE, HOUSTON POLISH INVESTMENT AND TRADE AGENCY

"*Manny Schoenhuber points out that since the US market is capitalistic and customer-based, it can be something of a safe haven for the experienced businessperson. Once one invests in the US business world, the potential for significant return on that investment is quite high. Mastering Market Entry: USA is a primer into diving into the US's all-the-time-growth market model in such a way that one enjoys the process while reaping the rewards that fuel the American Dream.*"

—PATRICK SCHOENOWSKI, CONSULTANT FOR ECONOMIC POLICY DEUTSCHER MITTELSTANDS-BUND (DMB) E.V. (GERMAN MITTELSTAND ASSOCIATION)

"*Don't let any lack of knowledge inhibit your company's growth. Mastering Market Entry: USA comes at the perfect time. It gives you a step-by-step process that eases some of your burdens of responsibility while preparing you for the American experience.*"

—IRENE LACK-HAGENEDER, COMMERCIAL ATTACHÉ AND HEAD OF ADVANTAGE AUSTRIA WASHINGTON, DC

"*Mastering Market Entry: USA convinces European companies that they can be a player in the US marketplace. Although many Europeans have serious misgivings about the prospect, they should follow Manny Schoenhuber's advice and complete the market entry journey. Reach out to your service providers and discuss Manny's strategies at length. Manny is available to be a lawyer on your team when you take your business to the US.*"

—ANDRÉ PANTEL, MANAGING DIRECTOR OF GERMAN-AMERICAN LAWYERS' ASSOCIATION (DAJV)

MASTERING MARKET ENTRY: USA

Mastering MARKET ENTRY: USA

The European's Guide to Making It **BIG** in America

Manny Schoenhuber

LIONCREST
PUBLISHING

MASTERING MARKET ENTRY: USA
The European's Guide to Making It Big in America

FIRST EDITION

ISBN   978-1-5445-4551-6 *Hardcover*
       978-1-5445-4553-0 *Paperback*
       978-1-5445-4552-3 *Ebook*

Disclaimer:

Yes, I am a lawyer. So, of course, I have to add a legal disclaimer and also inform you that reading this book does not create an attorney-client relationship. The ideas presented in this book are provided as general information and for educational purposes. They are not a substitute for professional advice. I also do not make any guarantee or other promise as to any results that may be obtained from using the content of this book. Before taking action, please consult with your team of professionals.

CONTENTS

BONUS STAGE: ELEVATE

"The American Dream, the dream of the land in which life should be better and richer and fuller for every man, with opportunity for each according to his ability or achievement. It is a difficult dream for the European upper classes to interpret adequately, and too many of us ourselves have grown weary and mistrustful of it. It is not a dream of motor cars and high wages merely, but a dream of a social order in which each man and each woman shall be able to attain to the fullest stature of which they are innately capable, and be recognized by others for what they are, regardless of the fortuitous circumstance of birth or position. No, the American Dream that has lured tens of millions of all nations to our shores in the past century has not been a dream of merely material plenty, although that has doubtless counted heavily. It has been much more than that. It has been a dream of being able to grow to the fullest development as a man and woman, unhampered by the barriers which had slowly been erected in older civilizations, unrepressed by social orders which had developed for the benefit of classes rather than for the simple human being of any and every class. And that dream has been realized more fully in actual life here than anywhere else."

—JAMES TRUSLOW ADAMS

INTRODUCTION

Some will say that the American Dream is dead, but they're dead wrong. The American Dream is alive and well, and it's waiting for you.

Admittedly, what exists now is a *Modern* version of the American Dream, one that evolved from the *Classic*, almost mythical story represented in people like my dad's uncle. After World War II, he left the same, small German town where I was born and raised and immigrated to the United States. As if in a movie, he received a Green Card at the US Consulate in Munich despite speaking no English, then boated across the Atlantic to arrive on Ellis Island. During those days, the country seemed to be handing out Green Cards like candy.

He found work at a department store, took English classes at night, made ends meet to afford his one-bedroom apartment, and saved up enough to start his own business. It was a cosmetics company named Aloise, a variation of his real name, Alois.

When my dad's uncle reached retirement age, he sold the business and, best of all, is still living well. Like so many other immigrants during the great waves of immigration into America, he found a land of limitless opportunity, built something for himself, and lived a dream life. It was a dishwasher-to-millionaire kind of story.

This story is no longer as readily possible, at least not for individuals. Now, it serves companies. The *Modern* American Dream has shifted, but it is still very much there for the taking.

THE *MODERN* AMERICAN DREAM

Global economic conditions are pointing a beacon directly at the opportunities in America. The country is, now more than ever, actively welcoming European businesses into its ever-growing economy. I see it every day with my clients. Companies looking to expand into the United States find that, when approached strategically, their American business often multiplies the value of its European parent company. In some cases, I've even seen market entry into the US save European businesses.

One of my clients is the epitome of the *Modern* American Dream. They are a recycling company headquartered in a somewhat small town in Denmark. Privately held, they first increased the capacity of their facility in Denmark—a country of 6 Million, a population smaller than Houston, the Texan city that headquarters their American subsidiary.

Their initial growth in Denmark was a logical move

because they were comfortable with their surroundings. Denmark is still Denmark, and they didn't have to change their strategy much or take on significant risk. But as globalization kicked in, they understood that, as the saying goes, if you're not growing, you're dying. To grow, they mitigated risk by crossing the border into Germany. Although a lot of Danes speak German, the executives of this company did not, so it was a slightly bigger risk, but still controlled due to the proximity. Their potential customer base grew by the size of Germany, roughly 80 Million. Their success in Germany took hold, and they eventually added a total of three facilities there.

With varying cultures, languages, and labor environments, each stage of the growth plan brought with it its own risks. However, they were strategic and conservative as they built themselves into a mid-tier company.

When looking for the next growth opportunity, the company came to a realization. They already dealt with customers outside of Europe, utilized English as the global language of business, and made deals in US dollars (the denomination of the global reserve currency). It became a no-brainer—expanding into the US was the next natural step. That's when they set up a plant in Houston, Texas.

Their American subsidiary scaled their revenue. Moving forward, the sky's the limit for this company. Eventually, they expanded by adding a facility in Portugal. With a strategic new location in Texas, they can access markets on both American coasts. A little bit further and they can tap into Canada and Mexico, serving the greater USMCA market. For them, expansion into

America doesn't just represent short-term growth for the company. It establishes a new foundation.

They are now poised to access a much larger, growth-based, and capitalistic market that benefits their superior European product. (Let's face it. European companies, with their eye on quality and engineering, tend to create superior products and services.) Their story of growth isn't dissimilar to many companies seeking continuous improvement and opportunities.

Like the *Classic* American Dream, the *Modern* version requires leaving one's comfort zone, arriving in a land of massive opportunity, being strategic about growth, and tapping into a wealthy and healthy market. The best part? This opportunity is available to you, too. This book will lay out a broad strategic plan—from a lawyer's perspective—that you and your company can utilize to fulfill your own *Modern* American Dream in a shifting global market.

THE SHIFTING GLOBAL MARKET

Right now, the lack of growth in the European market means America is somewhat of a safe haven. Unlike the more frugal European markets, the US market is consumer-based. America's capital-centric, all-the-time-growth economic model means a proper investment creates the potential for high returns. As a European myself, I can say, the same controlled optimism doesn't exist in Europe (unfortunately).

Like all Europeans, European business owners are facing new challenges. Europe is dealing with high inflation, excessive bureaucracy (or bureau-*crazy*!), costly energy, currency problems, lack of qualified labor, and unfavorable fiscal policies—just to name a few. Certainly, America faces these issues, too. But they pale in comparison to other markets. These factors are swallowing up European companies. If these European companies, many of which are mid-market champions with world-class products and services, are to survive and thrive, it becomes absolutely necessary to come to the US.

However, most companies underestimate their potential in America because the popular narrative says that only tech companies succeed in America. That's wrong. You can enter the American market with any product or service, even if you offer something as tried and true as recycling. It's not like America doesn't already have recycling companies. But because my Danish client offers world-class operational products and services, they are thriving in the competitive environment of America. The same opportunity awaits you.

But opportunity comes with unknowns. For many Europeans—particularly Central Europeans—economic growth means entering the American market for the first time. Most will approach this process without the proper preparation, stifling the new company or subsidiary by not putting their best foot forward.

What does the best approach look like? Contrary to the conservatism traditionally seen in Europe, it's generally best to be more aggressive and have a "can do" attitude in America. That approach is embodied in the most successful American companies. Nike's famous tagline, for example, is "Just do it." Uber's is "Move the way you want." The most successful European companies fully commit to the American market by committing to the American "can do" spirit. With careful strategizing, the upfront costs of entering the US market are worthwhile. For one, those costs are somewhat offset by comparatively less regulation and bureaucracy, and lower taxes.

Not only that, but there is less risk of volatility. In every direction you look—at the local, state, and federal levels—systems of checks and balances ensure that the market continues to run smoothly enough for protected success. But, of course, there is always risk. To mitigate that risk, the path is presented here in logical and straight-forward language.

What's more, you don't have to leave your European headquarters behind. Instead, your entry into America will solidify your importance to your local community.

COMMUNAL GROWTH

As I pull back the layers on market-entry strategies, you can infuse your keen sense of community into your expansion plans. That means being as tight-knit with your American counterparts as you are with your local community.

European companies that have a tremendous opportunity for growth—mid-market champions—are often within an hour or two of a metropolitan region, but are nonetheless, the primary employer of their village or small city of 50,000 to 100,000 people. There is a different sense of community, a different sense of belonging to the local area that sets them apart from the major, international corporations headquartered in cities like Munich, Paris, or Vienna.

I grew up in a village like this—a place where community combined with teamwork to create a sense of belonging. These are the values I was raised with. I was lucky enough to play football professionally before becoming a lawyer, so collaborating in a team environment is important and second nature to me. It's how I approach business. The sense of community you hope to hang onto will inform the insights I share with you.

If you are the manager, CEO, or owner of a European business, our shared priority is strengthening your company's contribution to your local community's growth and beyond.

For me, America was brand new once, too. I moved to the US without having visited before. I understand the mindset, challenges, and opportunities of companies and investors in Europe casting an eye across the pond for the first time. In other words, I speak European but am an American lawyer—arguably, the best of both worlds. I will act as your translator between cultures, languages, legal systems, and markets, and hope to be the partner in your success.

A POINT OF ENTRY

This is not a book about "how to print money in America." It will not help you make a great product or provide a market-changing service. If you belong to a European company, your product is already superior to most everything out there—at least from my professional experience representing European companies in the US.

Rather, this book offers a set of guidelines derived from my professional experience working with companies and their teams—accountants, bankers, insurance brokers, and others. Along with me, the lawyer, service providers are seeing thousands of European companies enter the American market, and this book acts as a survey of the most common strategies that significantly increase the likelihood of success. The beauty of my job is the fact that I get to see many different companies entering the US market, and I see what the successful ones are doing right and what the unsuccessful ones are doing wrong. Believe me, there is some kind of secret sauce to success in the US. Let me try to share that recipe with you.

Broken up into several stages—and organized in chronological order of transitional action—this book will detail a thoughtful point of entry into the American market.

- Stage 1: Evaluate
- Stage 2: Engineer
- Stage 3: Execute
- Bonus Stage: Elevate

Put together, these *Four Es of Market Entry*, as I call them, will be part and parcel of cultivating success in America. Stage 1 focuses on pre-entry market analysis and *evaluation.* Here, you can determine if you are suited for entry into the US market and, if so, identify your goals. Afterward, you will compare dead markets across the globe alongside the growth potential of the American market. Closing out this stage we'll discuss the misconceptions that prevent action. Why are so many Europeans hesitant? Why are these limiting beliefs mistaken? We will answer those questions and more.

In Stage 2, you will learn how to *Engineer* the best setup for successful market entry. Included in this is the importance of timing, assembling the right team of service providers, thinking about an exit strategy (if necessary), and optimizing your entity structure to protect your European holdings.

With the analysis and planning complete, Stage 3 turns toward the *execution* of your plan. This is where I help you translate the differences between the American market and the market you are used to. Hiring employees, sales, and marketing operate uniquely in the US, as you will learn. You will also come to understand the importance of thoughtful transatlantic management. Above all, this stage will teach you how to protect yourself and your assets through contract design and other liability-limiting practices. I promise you won't have to bet the farm to make it in America.

Those three stages should put your company on the growth path in the US. However, there is also a fourth, Bonus Stage included in this book—additional strategies and resources—to *Elevate* your business to the next level. In this stage, I will touch on alternative market-entry strategies—mainly, mergers and acquisitions. Additionally, from a lawyer's perspective, I will mention some tax and insurance-based concepts to bring to your Certified Public Accountant (CPA) and insurance broker, respectively. And finally, to keep your market-entry momentum on a path toward growth, I will provide you with a list of resources made up of trade associations and government agencies as well as a *Market Entry Checklist* you can use as your step-by-step guide throughout the entire market entry phase.

And that's what this is all about—growth. Right now, many European companies are asking themselves how they can improve their challenging economic circumstances. "This too shall pass" is not the right approach. The main question you have to answer concerns the future of your company: *How do you want to drive the business forward?* There is something you can do, and it starts with evaluating a possible market entry into the United States.

I'm on your team, and it is my pleasure to assist you on your journey to growth and prosperity in the US. Are you ready?

Let's get started with Stage 1: Evaluate.

ELEVATE | Introduction

EVALUATE

1. Why You?

2. Why the US? Why Now?

3. Many Europeans Are Hesitant. Why Are They Wrong?

4. Timing

5. Assembling the Team

ENGINEER

6. Entity Structure

7. Transatlantic Management and Hiring Employees

8. Liability, Products, and Contracts

9. Sales, Marketing, and Your Brand

10. Growth

EXECUTE

THE MARKET ENTRY JOURNEY

» Stage 1 «

Evaluate

WHY YOU?

"Germans have a love affair with the status quo."

—WOLFGANG ISCHINGER

Nobody is really comfortable with change. Often, the most attractive path is the path of least resistance. For us Europeans, and especially Germans like myself or Wolfgang Ischinger, traditionalism guides decisions about the future. Once we have achieved some level of success and strength, we can think that little recourse is needed to maintain that success. The status quo turns into a lack of growth. For many, this stasis then leads to shortfall and shrinkage. Just take the automotive industry as one example.

In Tesla, how was it that a startup American automaker was able to usurp the success of countless German brands seemingly overnight? In a phrase: changing with the times. Early on, German and other European automaker giants like Mercedes, Mini, Volkswagen, Jaguar,

Volvo, Porsche, BMW, Lamborghini, and Audi were almost belittling Tesla for making what they perceived to be risky moves. These companies were well-funded and already had their production facilities, the know-how, the engineering capabilities, and everything they thought they needed to keep their market share. So they stood pat and decided on inaction.

They felt secure in their combustion-engine product instead of pursuing the innovation of affordable electric and self-driving cars. But people wanted their cars to be computers. Tesla adapted, and now Teslas are everywhere. The Europeans are playing catch up, and meanwhile, heavily subsidized Chinese electric vehicles are also flooding the market.

In addition to a lack of innovation that prevented these European automakers from growing, it was also a bad overall strategic plan. For example, they only had limited capacity at their manufacturing plants in America, driving prices up and reducing their potential customer base in the US. This made things easier for Tesla, which utilized its California manufacturing plant to make the product where they sold it. Later, Tesla would cut costs even further by moving to Texas. Europeans, on the other hand, ship their electric vehicles and many of their combustion engine cars on costly boats and trucks before landing on the showroom floor. The Europeans are finally starting to catch on, with many of them seriously considering American manufacturing and others working on expansions of their existing plants on American soil due to various incentive programs, such as the Inflation Reduction Act. But not everyone is embracing change.

CHANGE IS NECESSARY

It's better to be late than never, but being stuck in your ways is at the cost of growth opportunities. Most Europeans don't like change, much to our business detriment. But you have to ask yourself one important question: *Do you want more?* It's time to *Evaluate* your situation—the first of the *Four Es of Market Entry*. If the answer is yes, then it's time to do something about it. Look in the mirror, and in that reflection, realize that you can do something about the direction you're heading. It's your duty. It's your job to create a more prosperous future. When you are in a position to expand your business, you also improve the situation for yourself, your employees, and your community. Do you want to be on the sidelines of change and stay satisfied with what you've already accomplished, or do you want to move forward and grow?

Change is inevitable. In the face of that change, have a clear understanding of the company's goals and how they align with your personal goals. Use those goals to drive your business forward through a thoughtful market entry using the strategies in this book. Evaluate your situation and the markets to see if expanding into America is right for you.

OVERVIEW OF THE EUROPEAN ECONOMY

The European companies I work with right now—those with a subsidiary in the United States—are receiving more orders from US customers than they get from anywhere else in the world. They are super busy. Business, right now, is booming. In Europe, things are different. There's stagnation in the European economy, and there aren't too many signs pointing toward growth. That fact alone should have you considering a move into the US market.

STAGNATION OR CONTRACTION

Europe has experienced growth over the years, no doubt. But it's getting to the point where a low-interest-rate environment has come to an end due to skyrocketing inflation. The very few European countries that drive Europe's larger economic growth, as well as the European Central Bank (ECB), are unable to raise interest rates quickly—unlike the Federal Reserve Bank of the United States—to fend off inflation.

If the ECB were to hike up interest rates, countries with a high debt burden would go belly up, like in 2010 when everybody had to step in to save Greece. But back then many other European countries had strong economies. Today, the German and French economies are contracting, and Britain is no longer part of the European Union. All of these factors come into play, and when looking at growth potential on paper, it's not really there.

Making matters worse is the disappearance of low-cost raw materials, energy, labor, and production and manufacturing. There are some hard-to-get government stimulus options out there, but at some point, European companies are having to foot a hefty bill.

THE DILEMMA OF QUALITY OF EUROPEAN PRODUCTS

Europe certainly faces a worrisome economic situation. But what is it that European companies have that is of value in other global regions? Product quality. Historically, European products have driven the European economy. Whether it's cars, chemical products, or engineering, it doesn't really matter. Europe stands for quality.

Despite this strength, warning lights are flashing. Continuing to rely on high-quality products while maintaining the status quo of business operations might not be enough anymore. Delivering those products means continuing to take on enormous costs that cannot be balanced with increasing sales. Driven by social and political factors, not the least of which is the Russian-Ukraine war and supply-chain issues, rising costs means you can't charge the same prices anymore. That runs the risk of getting priced out of your markets.

What's the solution? You can bring your quality product to the US *and* (if you wish) even manufacture it locally. Opening a local subsidiary reduces the need to change your prices due to shipping, import tariffs, and the like. The recently passed Inflation Reduction Act also incentivizes and subsidizes the manufacturing of certain locally sourced and manufactured products, such as electric vehicles. And although European companies have long stood for quality and innovation, they are falling behind the times, in terms of technological edge.

EUROPE'S TECHNOLOGICAL EDGE

Arguably, the current technological capitals of the world are Silicon Valley, Austin, and Seattle. What was once a hallmark of Europe—its technological edge—is no longer. The incentives for technological advancement in America are so strong, that startups and established companies have a dearth of choices. Fifty states mean fifty different sets of laws and regulations to implement for the most business-friendly situation. For example, Elon Musk's Tesla moved from California—the same state that Silicon Valley calls home—to Texas for legal, business, tax, and incentive purposes.

The grim state of affairs in Europe has moved some of its largest companies out west, a path that you should follow. Take SAP, a German company with the title of "largest non-American software company" (and third-largest in the world). They moved to California, where they opened up an American branch, and turned it into their cash cow. But just moving out west isn't enough. Even with that expansive mindset, SAP chose not to significantly innovate its software products, leaving market space to the Oracles and Salesforces of the world to eat away at its market share. As the chapters go along, we'll talk about how to avoid mistakes like that.

Of course, SAP will be fine. They are a huge, multinational conglomerate. But what about you and all of the European companies? If you choose to enter the US market, you can be more than fine. You already have a leg up; because Europe is part of America's history and tradition, you are already poised to succeed in the US. That's especially true if your expansion into the United States is done with strategic intention.

EUROPEAN COMPANIES ARE SUITABLE FOR THE US MARKET

American consumers—either individuals or businesses— know that Europe makes high-quality products. Whether that's "Made in Germany," "Made in Austria," "Made in Switzerland," or "Made in France," labels such as these strike the American consciousness as being of inherent quality, importance, and value. They are proud to use European products.

This reverence for European quality is found almost everywhere you look, and sometimes in extremely mundane ways. For example, one close American friend of mine loves to tell the same anecdote about eating bread in France. She swears that—in all of the luxury American breads she has sought—nothing has ever compared to the run-of-the-mill, gas-station baguette she bought in Grenoble, France. "Their gas stations have better bread than you'll ever have in your life," she loves to joke. Meanwhile, and this is a life tip if you don't know, the gas station food in America is mostly inedible—unless you ever make it to a Buc-ee's location. I highly recommend you treat yourself to this experience. As a European, you may be overwhelmed at first (like I was), but you may be pleasantly surprised. The important takeaway, however, is that what's true for her experience with bread is, by and large, true for America's view of European products.

This affinity for Europe extends beyond the virtues of its products. It stems from deep cultural ties to Europe as well as a love of its history. America, after all, is a country of immigrants, many of which came from Europe.

A COUNTRY OF IMMIGRANTS

America is known as a melting pot, an amalgamation of many different cultures and histories. Creating a soft landing for your market entry is the plain fact that America is heavily made up of European immigrants. There were great waves of Irish, German, and Norwegian immigrants, among others. My Dad's uncle was one among them. I've found that Americans are very proud of their heritage, whether it's European or something else. They take those trips to visit their ancestral home, to see the village where their great-grandparents were born and raised.

They are curious about where they came from, so much so that part of America's popular culture is devoted to mythically imagining Europe's past. The Walt Disney Company—the largest media company in the world—has made its money doing just this with films like *Snow White and the Seven Dwarves* (1937) all the way to *Frozen II* (2019). But it's not just one studio. For a time, Americans were obsessed with 20th Century Fox's *The Sound of*

Music. I don't have the heart to tell my American friends that not many people in Europe care about that movie or even know it. Full disclosure, I was born and raised near Salzburg and had not even heard about it until I came to the US.

I know one individual who loved the book and live-action series *Outlander*—a fictional story about Scotland by an American author—so much that she began traveling to Scotland once a year to visit featured landmarks. Think about that. People in the US are so captivated by Europe that they make up fictitious versions of it which then spurs travel plans.

Being European, in my experience, creates an easy connection; it bridges the gap perceived to exist between yourself and the market you plan on entering.

SPEAKING THE SAME LANGUAGE

Connections run deep between Europe and the US, including language.

Europeans are trained to be proficient in English, both spoken and written. Take me, for instance. I studied English at school in Germany and then, went to college in Florida, and ultimately, studied law in Texas. That's an extreme transfer of skills—not everybody will need to wield English so precisely as they do when studying law— but I was fully prepared by my European education system.

Certainly, some European countries are better at teaching it than others, but it's a central aspect of our education. You may come to find, too, that your English grammar is a little more, shall we say, rules-based than your average American. I often found myself cleaning up the punctuation on my American peers' papers in college and even my law firm colleagues frequently ask me to give their pleadings another look before submission, and they are so fascinated by it. I don't mean that as a slight by any means. Americans themselves are people of action and not necessarily rules, which can be a good thing. But, in terms of communicating with them, you have all the tools you need.

If you are doing international business, and you speak English, then America is next on the list of natural progression. You can speak to your customers in their own language. Even if you feel your English is not perfect, you'll be very well-equipped to do business in the US.

You don't have to fully understand a contract. That's why you hire a person like me—somebody fluent in both languages as well as lawyer-speak—to advise you and explain the legalese from an American point of view.

Your suitability for the market is no longer in question. But perhaps you are still concerned about how your goals in Europe might transfer to a prospective US subsidiary.

IDENTIFY YOUR GOALS

Part of the evaluation process for an entry into the US market is asking yourself what you want. What is it on the personal level and on the company level? And do you want growth? If so, you probably don't have many alternatives that are as risk-free, as we will explore in future chapters.

For now, what I will say is that, compared to the alternatives, the US aligns itself with European political and social goals. Sure, China can produce cheaply. But what if China decides to invade Taiwan tomorrow? As it and other BRICS countries become more and more reliant on a totalitarian system, the less they'll be driven by social values of communal good. In February of 2023, India, China, and South Africa all abstained from a UN vote condemning Russia's invasion of Ukraine. That pretty much tells you all you need to know.

Europe as a geographic region, and the European Union in particular, is a value-based union. We all share the same values. The credo of the EU is to strengthen relationships and to improve the welfare of each neighbor's life. Doing business in markets that don't align with those values becomes hypocritical and quite risky. How can we be saying one thing about sustainability, human rights, and other important global topics to only turn a blind eye when it comes to business?

While I don't condemn anybody for continuing to do business in countries that don't share our values, what I am saying is that you are opening yourself up to significant risk and volatility.

Ultimately, your goal is to grow. Everybody is trying to earn money, so why go cheap and risky when you can go sustainable? If you know you have a better chance of fulfilling your goals by investing in America, and you know you have a soft landing with a better product and a shared language, why wouldn't you be all-in?

In addition to sharing Europe's values, the US market

fosters entrepreneurship, is pro-growth, has less bureaucracy, and offers a reliable legal system and business environment. As your company grows, it can continue to grow by tapping into Canada and Mexico, eventually creating a launching-off pad for other places around the globe. That endless possibility for growth is part and parcel of the *Modern* American Dream.

You need to ask yourself critically—giving both the economic analytics and sociopolitical elements a hard look—where sustainable growth will be in the future. The answer to those inquiries is "America" every single time.

ALL ROADS LEAD TO AMERICA

There's really only one choice for European companies to expand to: America.

And that choice will be risk-mitigating. If you're doing it the right way, and you set up your entities properly, you won't be betting your entire European company. And, of course, you can always go back home, just like I told myself when I got on a plane before ever having visited the US.

It's the safer, sensible strategy to look to the US for growth. Many have done it before, and there's no reason you can't succeed, too. In fact, many of the companies I work with realize the process was relatively easy.

The road to America means exploring its system in more detail—its social values, economy, politics, and others. In chapter two, you'll learn that America is built on a foundation of strength, one that helps its economy thrive.

WHY THE US?

"Capital goes where it's welcome."

—WALTER WRISTON

In the evaluation process, identifying your own goals is an excellent place to start. Eventually, you need to move on and *Evaluate* your potential markets. In my mind, the only market worth evaluating is the US market—at least right now.

What makes the US economy stand apart from others? When looking to expand into new markets, many contemplate China, with a population of over a billion people. From a B2C point of view, a billion more potential customers sounds like a good idea.

More customers is a good thing but only if all of those customers have the freedom to buy your product or service while living in a society of checks and balances that looks out for the customers' best interests. Unideal customers are those living under a totalitarian regime that dictates its people's lives. When looking at places such as China or Russia, countries that are getting less democratic in their systems, an international company's ability to thrive there is largely handcuffed by the political moment.

In China specifically, companies usually have to enter into a joint venture with a Chinese-established company, meaning that the Chinese company could then infringe on your intellectual property without adequate recourse. Therefore, merely entering the Chinese market is akin to betting the farm. There's a reason why China encourages engineering and manufacturing companies to do business there: the true value of these companies is the intellectual property they have.

Rather than put yourself at risk, you need to pick an expansion country that is pro-growth, pro-entrepreneurship, and pro-freedom. That alternative is the United States.

Businesses succeed on their ability to generate capital—or revenue. Every investor in the world wants a return on their investment, just like a company has a responsibility to its shareholders or an owner to their family, employees, and community. And guess what? America calls it capitalism for a reason. They, like you, are focused on growing capital.

The fact of the matter is the US economy is the biggest economy in the world and is still growing. If that weren't enough to convince you, the US also has less governmental regulation and bureaucracy than many other places, thereby creating an environment that fosters innovation and ingenuity.

From a purely managerial perspective—from the desks

of the day-to-day decision makers and executives—it's important to look at the pros and cons of the US market. You should also do that before fully committing to entering the US market. In the end, I would argue that the pros outweigh the cons considerably, especially when compared with the alternatives.

The biggest "pro" of all, though, is the fact that the US engineers its system for sustainable growth.

SUSTAINED GROWTH IN THE US

Don't listen to European news that the United States is doomed because it's divided. To a certain extent, the division is an obvious truth. But it's not an alarming one. With just two major political parties, of course, it has division. But it also has democracy and capitalism. Therefore, the portrayal of America as coming apart at the seams is just not accurate, and it existed long before the Trump years. "American democracy is near the end," is the constant headline. Wrong.

What these narratives forget is the system's checks and balances. For example, there are divisions—there's that word again—of power equally among the executive, legislative, and judiciary branches of government. So, in that sense, the country uses division for its own growth and sustainability—the opposite of how its division gets covered by different European media outlets. The Supreme Court can shift conservatively for now, but that will be met by a liberal congress. Within Congress, the House may lean one way while the Senate the other.

The stewards of these bodies of power are always shifting. It will always be a system where folks without political allegiances will have to work together to find bipartisan common ground. The system itself fosters collaboration, negotiation, and a desire to work together in an equally compromising partnership. Because of this innate need for collaboration, no single element of this system—not even the President—can screw things up so badly that it might bring democracy to an end in this country.

In the immediate aftermath of the January 6 Riots, European media pointed to the event as the death knell for the democratic experiment. But look at those who participated now. Most of them are in jail and were handedly taken care of by a combination of the Department of Justice and the Judiciary. The US legal and government systems functioned properly and will continue to do so.

And in the event that every major body of power, such as the House, the Senate, the Presidency, and the Supreme Court (let's just stay in the federal government for simplicity), might be held by the same party, there are offset election cycles. If supermajorities become unpopular, the country adapts by sussing it out, voting again, and reassessing the law. The two years one party might hold *all* power is not nearly enough to screw up the system, at least in my opinion.

All of that ignores something that most Europeans forget: individual states hold much of the legislative power. Why is it that businesses are flocking to Texas and Florida, so much so that some are even leaving California and New York? State legislatures. Again, the capital goes where it's treated best.

A major problem with the European perspective is that it's so focused on the coasts. BBC has its American affiliate in New York, while other major European media outlets are headquartered in places like Washington, DC, or San Francisco. It's easy to forget that there's a whole country in the middle. New York, in its own way, is an entirely different place—almost its own country—compared to middle-of-nowhere Texas. In turn, each state has its own, unique market.

US AND EUROPEAN MARKETS

A misconception many executives in Europe have about America is that their country's market is similar to or the same as the US market. This undermines a true understanding of the potential that market entry into the United States represents.

One Danish company I represent presumed that the US and Denmark were the same markets, and therefore, it shouldn't be so expensive to do business in America. Further, they believed that because of the similarities in Western culture, they wouldn't need any Danish representation at the US subsidiary. In both instances, in my professional opinion, they were incorrect.

Despite many similarities, the two worlds couldn't be more different. Although Denmark is not a socialist country, there is a much bigger emphasis on paying premium taxes to fund the common good, such as universal healthcare, than in America. In the US, we generally pay less taxes and reward companies more for taking on risk.

After that, it becomes simple math. At the time of this writing, Denmark is a country of 6 Million people. The US has 332 Million people. Denmark has one time zone compared to America's four continental time zones. America is bigger in more ways than one, and the economic output of *more* will be more substantial, as will the cost to invest.

Without proper transatlantic management, goals, operations, and perspectives will all radiate from these fundamental differences to create a disconnect between the European parent company and the US entity.

Those cultural differences are vast, and to succeed in America, you need to adopt an American mindset. One of my former football coaches in Germany may have said it best, "In America, if Michael Jordan's neighbor sees him pull up in a Ferrari, the neighbor is bound to applaud him and say, 'Well done! I'm happy for you. You earned it and deserve it! You worked really hard.' In Europe, if a neighbor saw Michael Jordan pull up in a Ferrari, Jordan would be lucky to still have all four wheels on his car the next day." What I think my coach tried to convey in a somewhat extreme way is that in Europe, there's a general sense that everybody should be the same. That my neighbor should not have more than I have. In America, on the other hand, the sense is that you should work hard to separate the quality of your service or product from the rest—and be rewarded for that effort.

This attitude, in part, helps strip away much of the needless bureaucracy found in many European systems.

MATTERS OF *BUREAU-CRAZY*

European companies often complain about how getting anything done in Europe takes way too long. The bureaucracy demands enough man-hours to act as an obstacle for expansion, especially for mid-tier companies. Of course, bigger companies, like Siemens and BMW, are wealthy enough to have their own, in-house legal and compliance officers handling the local bureaucracy.

When there's a tweak or change in labor laws, accounting, or any other standardized process, these big companies can roll with the punches because they have staff on the payroll sorting that out. Mid-market companies, on the other hand, don't have the resources to keep up with the constant bureaucratic changes. This challenge is then compounded when the mid-market company has to battle the EU standards on one side and their local market's standards on the other.

In many ways, European companies are being held back by the rules and regulations of the EU. Although they are poised for growth, as may be the case with your company, the circumstances naturally work against breakthroughs in revenue and expansion. This bureaucratic slog makes market entry into the US all the more obvious.

I'm not saying that America doesn't have bureaucracy. It does. But, relative to what you're used to in Europe, the US system will feel like you've been freed from a cage. You can actually focus on how to manufacture and sell your product or service.

In my experience, European companies are surprised by how quickly things actually get done in America. It does depend on which state we choose for the US company, but by and large things get done faster here. It's because the US appreciates and encourages entrepreneurship and innovation.

THE US FOSTERS ENTREPRENEURSHIP, BUSINESS, AND INVESTMENTS

The American reality television series, *Shark Tank*, is essentially the American business world in microcosm. Each business industry has its area of the country where startup and venture capital thrive. Silicon Valley is the center of the universe for tech. Houston is the center of the universe for energy, space, and the medical field. Wall Street is the center of the universe for banking and finance.

There's a reason all of these powerhouse economic forces set up shop in the US and are not in Europe or elsewhere. This has always been a country of entrepreneurs. There's a reason why the *Classic* (and *Modern*) American Dream has been associated with prominent entrepreneurs. It's the country of the Rockefellers, the JP Morgans, and those individuals whose vision and tenacity drove global economic growth.

But that entrepreneurial spirit extends beyond the individuals with capitalistic dreams. Federal, state, and local tax incentives, foreign direct investment grants, and other programs welcome entrepreneurs of all backgrounds to startup and see what they can do. In general, the American answer to every challenge is, "Yes, let's do that and figure out along the way how it can be done."

When there are roadblocks in America—such as processing the environmental rights of land targeted for expansion—that process is much more efficient and business-friendly than it is in Europe. In Europe, the first answer is usually, "No"—or even worse, "No, we can't do this because we've never done it before," or "No, because we've always done it another way."

THE ROLE OF THE US FEDERAL GOVERNMENT

Generally speaking, one of the top goals of the Federal Government is to foster investment in the US for economic development, whether the stock market, specific industries, or specific sectors of the economy. This creates an opportunity for the *Modern* American Dream to anybody working hard enough and doing the right thing.

In the last few years, these priorities have only intensified. The challenges the world faced during the COVID-19 pandemic—lack of material availability, high costs, and broken supply chains—created a need for not only growth but sustainable growth. Within that realization was the need to bring the global economy into the local markets. Given the shortages and supply-chain issues that the US faced during that time, there has been an initiative that production should be "near-shored," bringing manufacturing back home instead of importing from abroad. Rather than import cars on ships, economically encourage the automakers to set up shop on American shores to manufacture them here.

The Buy American Act, the CHIPS Act, and the Inflation Reduction Act all drive just what I'm talking about.

They welcomed capital investment in the country and made it worthwhile for European companies. For example, the Volkswagen Group now plans to open up two more plants based in the US in order to take advantage of the incentives.

Both pieces of legislation are at the federal level. There are even more business-friendly laws and incentives at the state and local levels.

THE ROLE OF STATE AND LOCAL GOVERNMENTS

Like the federal government, state and local governments have essentially the same pro-business goals. Texas, for example, provides companies with all kinds of incentives for setting up their headquarters in the state. Coming from the governor's office, that's a state policy. But where within the large state of Texas might a company want to open for business? That's a question your lawyer (familiar with US federal, state, and local laws) can help you answer. It's my job to help my clients suss out the relative pros and cons of municipalities like Houston, Dallas, Frisco, Austin, and other cities that each have their own local laws, incentive programs, and ordinances that may benefit a given company.

For example, energy companies usually do better in Houston or Dallas but not as well in Austin. On the other hand, a software company usually thrives in Austin. Each local government passes laws to benefit businesses that they want to attract and nurture. If Dallas has 5 percent rebates for a decade but Houston has 6 percent, that information will be vital to your choosing Houston. Be careful about your choice. Throwing a dartboard at a map of the US won't get it done.

An additional word of caution: don't commit to a specific location *before* asking for incentives. I have seen it before. A European company committed to setting up shop in the Greater Houston region first and then reached out to the local economic development organization (EDO) asking for incentives. Unfortunately, that's too late. You want to reach out to the EDO *before* you commit to a region. Let different areas enter into a bidding war for your business. Then, you can pick your favorite location after having secured the best overall package for your US location. Your lawyer should be able to facilitate the entire process for you.

THE VALUE OF US CURRENCY

Most European companies already sell globally and outside of the Eurozone. For those companies, they already trade using the US dollar, the global reserve currency. It's a natural progression, then, to go to a country where you already have familiarity with the currency. That is a far less risky proposition than entering into a country that will trade in its own, more volatile currency. If you have to trade in, let's say, the Japanese yen or the South African rand, you'll have to deal with the currency runs that affect their value (which means less predictable revenue). Not only that, but you'll need to hire new accountants and potentially change the bookkeeping system.

Where currency differences are something to keep in mind, so are other differences, such as time zones.

TIMEZONES AND THE EUROZONE

Although a comparatively minor benefit of doing business in the United States, the time difference across the country is not as bad as doing business in China or Japan where people might need to be waking up in the middle of the night to jump on the videoconference. In fact, many European companies will set up shop on the East Coast believing it to be the most advantageous timezone. However, Texas and many parts of the Midwest are only one hour behind the East Coast. So it's not that difficult to do business over the vast majority of the country. Now, California and the West Coast get a little more complicated for Europeans. But, in total, you will be able to conduct same-day business with easy access.

THE SKILLED US WORKFORCE

A perfect pairing for growing your business is the skilled US workforce combined with European ingenuity. We'll cover that premise in more detail in a future chapter.

For now, let's look at the wind energy industry as an example. Because of Texas' success with onshore wind energy (it's the leading producer of wind energy in the US[1]), governments are now also looking to attract offshore wind on both coasts as well as on the Gulf of Mexico. Many of those contracts are being awarded to US sub-

---

[1]   "Energy Is Good For Texas," Texas Comptroller of Public Accounts, accessed November 30, 2023, https://comptroller.texas.gov/economy/economic-data/energy/2023/wind-snap.php#:~:text=In%202023%2C%20wind%20represented%2028.6,coal%2Dfired%20generation%20in%202020.

sidiaries of European companies. The winning engineers, designers, and firms are all from across the pond.

One German client of mine that services the wind industry is bringing many of their technicians over from Germany to educate the American workforce here as those workers are just coming out of trade schools. This is true with other companies and wind or solar farms. Right now, the trend is that the European skills and products (and their quality) are winning the contracts, but these ingenuities are easily transferable to the American subsidiary's workforce, which proves to be highly skilled to carry out the parent company's goals.

No matter how you slice it—market size, skilled workforce, the business-friendly legislation, the lack of bureaucracy, or the friendly timezones—the US economy is growing. Better yet, it is encouraging European companies to join in on the growth.

WHY NOW?

The mindset in Europe as it faces economic challenges seems to be waiting and hoping. You'll hear things like, "Someday soon everything will be fine." That is a foolish risk to take, in my opinion. Why stand pat and simply hope that your company can survive? What if, in five years, sh** hits the proverbial fan and the economy doesn't recover as the "hope and pray" method suggests?

It's like the stock market. When it goes up, everybody makes money. During a tough trading period, you can see who's been swimming naked. In order to sustain a company through growth, one must be proactive. Do you want to make proactive decisions to help ensure a prosperous future? Now is the time to take a step toward growth in the US. The circumstances in Europe—economically, politically, and otherwise—are too risky.

Right now, there's a perfect storm taking the best investments toward America.

When Russia decided to invade Ukraine, Europe was in a bind because it received 80 percent of its natural gas from Russia. While this is only one resource, it can be said that economies are energy-dependent. By putting all of its eggs in one basket, the economy is screwed when that lifeline is lost. That's why it took so long for the EU to stop importing gas directly from Russia as part of its overall sanctions to protest against the legality of the war.

Prior to the war, I used to warn my family and friends back home in Germany. I would ask them how many liquefied natural gas (LNG) terminals there were in Germany to handle the country's needs if they suddenly weren't able to import cheap Russian gas through pipelines. The answer? Zero. Zero LNG terminals. They scrambled to build one as quickly as possible. In order to develop sustained economic growth, you need reliable sources of affordable energy. And arguably, Europe doesn't have that, at least in the short term. Most likely, the comparably high costs of energy will stick for the foreseeable future. Fortunately, they are developing long-term solutions now, but the late start means it's not the place to find immediate growth solutions.

In the US, the economic outlook is pretty much the

opposite. Yes, everybody is talking about inflation and recessions, but compared to what's happening in Europe, it's child's play. Operating within the US for my own work, all I see is that everybody is keeping busy, especially my clients. If any recession does hit, it will probably be a lot shorter than 2008. Regardless, recessions in the US are always historically shorter than in Europe, meaning that growth and rebound even in the face of a recession threat means that the US is a more advantageous market to enter.

The US actually faces economic challenges head-on, fostering business growth through legislation like the Inflation Reduction Act. Additionally, local municipalities offer their own forms of incentives to do business locally in the US. Take Samsung, for example, which just recently invested $17 Billion near Austin for their semiconductor program. This was the largest single instance of foreign direct investment (FDI) in American history until TSMC, the world's largest semiconductor company, announced an investment of $40 Billion at its US site in Phoenix shortly thereafter. If the US is good enough for them, chances are the US is good enough for your company, especially if you're looking to sell your products to North American customers.

In fact, the United States is home to the world's most FDI inward stock, which is a measurement used to show the linked strength of economies. In 2021, it totaled nearly $5 Trillion. What's more, European businesses made up over 56 percent—more than $3 Trillion—of FDI inward stock, showing that European companies see the value in doing business here.[2] Of that number, manufacturing, finance, insurance, information, and wholesale trade make up the largest investments.

Within that figure, European countries are increasing their investment in the United States. Austria, Germany, Denmark, Luxembourg, and Ireland are among the fifteen fastest-growing sources of FDI in America. Overall, German investments account for $636 Billion of FDI, the largest of any European country. In other words, the secret about America is out. How will you respond?

Beyond the business-friendly environment in the US, don't forget that there are no plans within the country to turn away business opportunities to allies with the same values. On the other hand, when other countries run afoul of international law, as ordained by the United Nations, that volatility results in harsh economic consequences. That fact hits close to home for me.

My father is an engineer for a large German engineering firm. As a site manager, he oversees and builds chemical plants and other refineries. He was head of a project located in Russia when Russia invaded Ukraine. Three weeks later, the EU blocked those projects and forced his company out of Russia. Russia, previously a huge market for my father's company, is now off the table. Where are they looking and investing now? The US and Canada. The company knows that there is less volatility in those markets, markets with checks and balances rather

---

2   "Direct Investment by Country and Industry," The U.S. Bureau of Economic Analysis, July 21, 2022. https://www.bea.gov/news/2022/direct-investment-country-and-industry-2021.

than a single, head-of-state decider. By the way, guess who stepped in to take over the job on all of their projects in Russia, including my Dad's project? Companies from China.

You, too, should carefully consider the potential dangers of investing in volatile markets such as the BRICS countries.

THE FUTURE OF BRICS

The BRICS countries (Brazil, Russia, India, China, and South Africa) are internationally recognized as having major economic potential. Many argue that, whether in ten, twenty-five, or fifty years, one or two of them may be able to overtake the US as the biggest economy in the world. Frankly, I don't see that happening.

The claim is that these countries offer growth opportunities. However, investments could go poorly rather quickly. Many of them perpetrate human rights violations, have a lack of democratic values, and fester with other significant social and political conflicts.

The opportunity for growth may be there, but it exists with an understanding that the rug can be pulled out at any moment. These countries do not have the US's stable and complex system of checks and balances. These countries do not have a capitalist-centric infrastructure designed to thoughtfully attract business and investment. The US does.

YOU'RE POSITIONED FOR SUCCESS IN THE US

Everything we've covered in this chapter makes one thing clear: you can succeed in the US Market. Does that mean you're now free of doubts, either from yourself, company ownership, or the board of directors? Of course not. Any market entry process needs thoughtful due diligence that carries with it some form of hesitation.

In the next chapter, we'll (un)cover the common hesitations that prevent Europeans from taking advantage of the growing US economy. After exposing them, I'll provide the ammunition to confront company leadership (or yourself) with the counterpoints to those limiting thoughts.

MANY EUROPEANS ARE HESITANT, AND HERE'S WHY THEY'RE WRONG

"If you are interested, you'll do what's convenient. If you are committed, you'll do whatever it takes."

—JOHN ASSARAF

Everybody's *interested* in growth. But it takes more than mere interest to actually grow. The same is true for businesses. Convenience, comfort, and overly conservative business choices usually lead to the absence of growth and, in some cases, to losses.

The hesitancy of many European businesses to enter the US market is driven mostly by fear. Many of them still remember the hot coffee lawsuit against McDonald's in 1994. McDonald's was sued for product liability after a customer spilled hot coffee on themselves. The jury awarded the plaintiff nearly $3 Million in damages because McDonald's failed to put a warning label "Caution Hot" on the coffee cup. Many mid-tier companies couldn't afford such a loss, and the perceived frivolousness of the lawsuit made many parts of the world believe the US was a legal Wild West where anybody could receive a windfall for anything.

My professional experience demonstrates such fears are mostly unfounded. It's time to round out the first of the *Four Es of Market Entry* by *evaluating* what makes Europeans hesitant in order to dispel the most common fears and to encourage you to enter the US market.

FEAR OF LITIGATION AND BANKRUPTCY

When European clients come to me, by a substantial margin their biggest fear is litigation. They are afraid of getting sued in the US. I hear the same story from bankers, accountants, insurance brokers, and other service providers I regularly work with. It is so prevalent that there even is a fancy name for it: *liticaphobia*—the irrational fear of lawsuits. Compounding that fear is the dual cost of litigation. There's the cost of losing a lawsuit, but there are also the fees for the professionals working on your behalf. This is because the "American Rule" requires that opposing parties in a lawsuit each pay their own attorneys' fees, whether they win or lose the case. There are contractual and statutory exceptions to the American Rule, and you should discuss these with your lawyer. But, in any event, when it all adds up, the fear of litigation is really a fear of losing the entire business.

There's a perception out there that if people can sue McDonald's for spilling hot coffee, it has to be an overly litigious country. It is true, to a certain extent. Annually, more lawsuits are filed in the US than in any other country. However, the moniker of "most lawsuits per capita" has historically belonged to Germany.[3] So, from a strictly mathematical standpoint, a German company has a greater chance of being sued in their own country than in America.

Nonetheless, there are ways to properly protect your parent company from lawsuits in America. I'll go into more detail in later chapters, but a solid foundation and basic rule is to never do business in the US with your European entity—putting all of your assets in one entity keeps your company's assets exposed to litigation. Just one separate US entity can protect your European parent company.

Working with your team—lawyers, bankers, insurance brokers, and accountants—can shore up a proper entity structure, which is a huge part of what is needed to put your mind at ease, as far as litigation is concerned.

Even if the worst happens and you have to fold your cards because you can't pay a court judgment against your company, bankruptcy isn't the end of the road. There's

---

3   Christian Wollschläger. *Exploring Global Landscapes of Litigation Rates, Soziologie des Rechts: Festschrift fur Erhard Blankenburg* 582 (1998).

adversity toward bankruptcies in Europe—that failure means a stain on the reputation of your business acumen and any future work. In the US, it's pretty common and generally not frowned upon. In America, creditors understand the importance of reorganization.

To a certain extent, the failure associated with bankruptcy is actually sought after in America. It means you are actively trying to get better. How do I know this? Here's just one example. A German friend of mine who is also the CEO of a German company's US subsidiary was looking into joining various advisory boards for other American companies. Nobody, however, would accept him simply because he has no setbacks on his resume.

Unlike Europeans, Americans love a good comeback story; lifting yourself up from failure is an important part of success in the US. Just take Tiger Woods. While at the top of his game, he dealt with a slew of injuries and personal issues that derailed his career in the early 2010s. Accepting those challenges and continuing to work toward success, he won the 2019 Masters Tournament. That win was lauded as one of his best considering the struggles he had previously faced. Failure is never the end of the story here. If you fail, make sure you fail forward.

I've lived, studied, and worked in America now for many years. Although it was risky, and I had some underlying fears, I had a comforting thought—I would still have my family and friends in Germany. If things didn't work out for me, I could always go back home. The safety of an exit strategy is available to your company as well. With the proper entity structure, if the American subsidiary goes under (for any reason, including litigation), then so be it. You can always go back home, reorganize, or start a new US venture.

As you will clearly understand as the book unfolds, you won't be betting your entire business without taking precautions.

Ultimately, I also tell my clients that getting sued is not the end of the road and even somewhat of a compliment in the US. If you're doing things the right way, you will only get sued if you're successful. The plaintiff's lawyer— whether that lawyer represents a terminated employee, a rival company suing for patent or trademark infringement, or something else entirely—will only file a lawsuit if they know there's money to be had. Otherwise, a mere "paper judgment" against a judgment-proof company wouldn't be worth the lawyer's time and resources.

And what do I mean when I say that you do things the right way? Let's take Volkswagen again. Just recently, they screwed up big time. They were knowingly cheating the system by lying about the cleanliness of their diesel cars. After going to court, they had to pay damages as well as penalties, and frankly, they deserved to be dragged into court. When you are not trying to cheat somebody and you do things the right way, lawsuits tend to stay out of your purview. If you don't cheat, you usually don't need to be afraid of litigation.

There are times, however, when European companies need to take a stance and actually have to file a lawsuit so that they are not being taken advantage of. Again, it's about adapting to the US market environment, which demands filing lawsuits to put pressure on the other party. Much more so than we are used to in Europe. In Europe, lawsuits are usually a last resort. In the US, we file lawsuits relatively quickly to get heard.

If fear of litigation is essentially a fear of cost, what other aspects of the US market make folks balk? The cost of operation.

FEAR OF COST OF OPERATION

In my experience, the cost of operation is the number two fear European companies face when considering an entry into the US market.

Things are expensive in the United States; no doubt about that. We can look at any aspect of business operations. For the sake of ease, let's look at service providers like me, the lawyer. Folks like me sell our time, not a product. European companies are often shocked at how much service providers in the US charge for their time. Accountants, lawyers, you name it. Because of this, companies will try to look for the cheapest options, sometimes even foregoing getting any advice from professionals.

In the face of these kinds of cost-cutting measures, let's conduct a thought experiment. Let's say a company wants to save some money by signing a contract without letting its lawyer review it first. The company saved maybe $5,000 to $10,000 in legal fees. Over the course of fulfilling the contract, there was some disagreement between the parties about its nuances. Things get heated, and the contract-signing company gets sued for breach of contract, loses millions of dollars, and has to start again from scratch. At the end of this story—one I have seen occur many times—the cost of not using service providers far outmatched the perceived initial savings.

Saving a few bucks in America means opening yourself up to unnecessary vulnerabilities. Closing those vulnerabilities means accessing the upside of the American market.

Here's a game-changing tip to help you manage the high costs: price them into your product or service being sold in the US market. That should be easy to do whether you sell million-dollar construction projects or thousands of small widgets. One of my European clients sells drinking straws, a small, inexpensive product that one would think can only be competitively priced if you cut every corner. Well, even they managed to price their legal review and contract costs into the product offerings.

It's a mathematical and business mistake to simply convert the Euro price you sell your product for in the Eurozone into US dollars for sale in America without factoring in market differences. The costs to enter and operate within the American market will affect your product's price. Americans are willing to pay more, by and large, because they also participate in that larger-scale economy. Plus, your product is likely already of higher quality, meaning that Americans are already more willing to pay a premium for it.

Here's some advice when it comes to your legal fees: find a lawyer who is reasonably priced. I'm not saying you should spend $1,000 or more per hour as many US lawyers charge. I, for example, use a pricing model that is similar to the European market and the going hourly rates there. That's because my goal is to build long-term business relationships with my clients and not a quick transactional relationship. I also encourage my clients to discuss pending invoices with me, and we usually come to a resolution that works for everyone, thus centering the discussion on building a long-term relationship instead of making a quick buck. My clients value my European approach and pricing model, and at the same time, enjoy the benefits of a true full-service law firm.

Yes, costs are higher in the US. And, as has been said, Germans (and maybe even most Europeans) have a love affair with the status quo. It's something you may have to overcome personally rather than through a business plan or otherwise. Your company, over generations, may have grown into 50 or 100 Million euros in annual revenue. That wouldn't even get you close to showing up on the list of Fortune 500 companies in the US. In other words, adapt and be willing to realize that change is not only necessary for growth, but it can lead to scaling growth in the world's greatest economy.

FEAR OF DIFFERING LEGAL SYSTEMS

Europeans aren't often aware of how starkly different their legal systems are from the US system. That in and of itself creates a mystery, a gap of knowledge that begets a fear of market entry.

For those who stay blissfully unaware and still decide

to enter the US market, they make strange choices. For one, they'll translate their Terms and Conditions from their home country's language into American English believing that it will translate just fine. They don't. You need service providers like lawyers and CPAs to advise on all matters legal and tax.

Generally speaking, most European countries use a legal system based on *civil codes*. Belgium and Luxembourg, for example, base theirs on the *French Code Civil* or *Napoleonic Code*. That means codes or statutes dictate most legalities. That's why these countries have these big law books filled with codes. I'm sure you've seen some of those statutory law books. They're massive.

On the other hand, US law (by and large) is based on British *common law*. In America, cases and laws are decided based on legal precedence, the nuances between differing laws, and the structure of laws in different jurisdictions. Further, US common law is such where statutes and codes don't readily determine legal outcomes. Instead, courts decide based on the legal choices that have come before, representing a commonality among legal implementations.

Merely understanding that legal differences exist is the first step to overcome this hesitancy. Beyond that, educating yourself is the next step. Best of all is having a trusted lawyer on your team who can provide expert and professional advice on the differences in law between the country of your parent company and the US jurisdiction of your subsidiary. It might be a more expensive cost upfront, but it will pay dividends later.

As I tell my clients, it's my job to translate not only between languages but also between legal systems. I try to guide them through the US legal landscape and all its common law peculiarities that are still "uncommon" to most Europeans.

So far, you will have noticed, all of these market-entry hesitancies are grounded in a fear of not being protected if things go wrong. To alleviate those fears, I suggest you rely on the *Three Pillars of Limiting Liability*.

THE THREE PILLARS OF LIMITING LIABILITY

Fears and misconceptions lead to missteps. With enough missteps—whether from stagnation, forging ahead without the proper advice, or analysis paralysis—the walls of your company will crumble.

Instead, you need to build yourself a resilient structure that, like Roman architecture, will last. To do so, let me introduce you to the *Three Pillars of Limiting Liability*. In order of importance, they are Entities, Contracts, and Insurance.

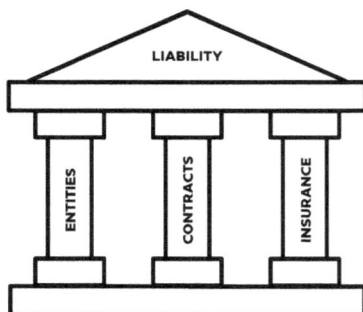

If you build these *Three Pillars*, the weight that is liability will be held at a distance from your assets and company. You will be protected, and your hard work won't come crashing down to the ground because of the accumulation of missteps eroding the foundation of your work.

Although I will go into more detail on each pillar throughout the book, let's briefly go over each to acquaint ourselves with their basic premises. I start with *Entities* as the first pillar of limiting liability because, quite simply, your choices as to entity structure and setup will ripple consequences outward for every future move you make. That seems daunting now, but there are ways to set up your entities to protect your American assets, your European assets, and your personal assets. This includes separating them so that, in the event of litigation, folks cannot go after a business-breaking amount of money.

With the *Entities* in place and the company ready to do business, the second pillar of limiting liability involves creating air-tight *Contracts*. Whether they relate to customers, product disclaimers and warranties, employment agreements, or another type of written agreement, the language and design you implement will have far-reaching effects on your ability to protect your company and yourself from liability. That's because, in the US legal system, we generally enjoy the *freedom of contract*—the ability of parties to bargain and create the terms of their agreement as they desire without outside interference from the government or regulators.

Afterward, we require *Insurance*—the third pillar of limiting liability—to ensure that we can take care of any litigation event or accident. I'll cover your relationship with your insurance broker briefly in Chapter 5. But because I am a lawyer and not a broker, my "take these ideas to your broker" advice will appear later, in the Bonus Stage: Elevate near the end of the book.

Without exception, you need to build each pillar with care. Doing so will further assist you in eliminating any hesitations you may still have about US market entry.

EXCUSES

When I played professional football in Germany, my coaches were full of sage advice. One thing one of my coaches repeatedly said to us was that "excuses are like a**holes because everybody has one and they all stink." He called us out on our excuses and forced us to take responsibility, admit our failures, and take charge of our futures by not taking the easy way out.

If you are committed to growing your company through US market entry, you'll do whatever it takes, no excuses. It's not about putting yet another book down with a plan for tomorrow or getting stuck in analysis paralysis. It's about starting right now and taking charge. That's what this book is all about—a call to action!

The theory is done. Congratulations! Evaluating why you should enter the US market is over. It's clear that the US economy offers European companies the opportunity to grow. Now it's time to *Engineer* that growth by picking the right place and the right time for your company's

US market entry. You and your company are destined for growth in the US if you do things the right way.

The next part of the book is about putting the plan together to take full advantage of what the US market has to offer all while protecting your company and yourself against risk.

Let's move on to Stage 2: Engineer.

» Stage 2 «

Engineer

TIMING

"There is no time like the present."

—JOHN TRUSLER

I hate to state the obvious, but the US market is not waiting for you. The US economy will be just fine. However, you will need the US right now to grow and take your company to the next level. It's time we move to the second of the *Four Es of Market Entry: Engineer.* Let's take the necessary steps to *Engineer* a smooth and successful entry into the US market for you and your company.

As the first actionable step, we need to carefully suss out the timing of your market entry. Don't come with an approach that is incomplete, too early, or too late. Don't get caught up in analysis paralysis and unnecessarily delay your arrival. So many people look for that additional piece of confirmation, but don't let excessive due diligence slow you down.

Always look at the complete picture. Who knows, your research may show it's not the right time. Take Peter Diamandis, whose 2012 startup, Planetary Resources, sought to harvest resources from asteroids. At the time, famed entrepreneur Elon Musk praised the startup as having a great idea, but cautioned it was several decades too early since the technology to achieve such a feat was less than readily available (it wasn't even theoretically available). Musk's prediction proved true. By 2020, Planetary Resources had been purchased with its assets subsequently auctioned off. And Peter Diamandis readily admits that Musk was right.

The lesson at the heart of Diamandis' story is that timing is a reality check. Although the US market sustains growth right now, you need to understand the circumstances by which you can make the best-timed entry into the US market.

Often, it can be more helpful to learn something by considering what *not* to do. Before we get to the circumstance of perfect timing, I'll start with the red flags that may indicate you are either too early or too late.

TOO EARLY

There are many factors that may indicate you are, in fact, too early. Although the US economy is a place for growth for European companies, and it is my advice to enter that market as soon as possible, there are steps that, when ignored, might mean you are entering the market prematurely.

NO PROOF OF CONCEPT AND NO FUNDING

Software companies are the biggest contributors to this "too early" mistake. They are tech companies, app developers, or engineers with a theoretical product. Just three weeks before I began writing this book, a startup subsidiary of a European company contacted me with hopes of soliciting advice on funding. It was a med-tech company. They didn't have any prototypes or proof of concept yet, just (really good) ideas. In fact, they sought funding merely from a pitch deck. They wanted to raise $4 Million, which makes it quite difficult because such a comparably low amount is hard to raise—even in the US. Actually, in the US, you are usually better off asking for more. Even worse, their parent company had nothing of significance invested to provide seed funding. In other words, they had no real skin in the game. That's a giant red flag for all potential US investors—whether private equity, venture capital, or accredited private investors.

The European narrative is that the entire US has a Wall Street atmosphere with limitless opportunities and stacks of money ready to be handed out. But that's not how it actually works. Further, as funding tightens up in the US a little bit, you can't expect venture capital, private equity, or even private investors to line up and hand you money, much less meet with you—especially if you don't have a product and the company itself has not invested much.

To successfully enter the US market, you have to have your product made, ready to ship, and already show signs of proven success.

When those elements align and you do have proof of

concept, your timing is good. You'll be on better footing, funding-wise, if you can demonstrate you are an investable company in the here and now.

HAVEN'T FOUND SUCCESS IN EUROPE

If you haven't tested (with proof of success) your product or service in Europe, it's not likely the US will welcome you with open arms. You're probably too early.

Ask yourself this simple question: *Have you found success in Europe with the product or service that you hope to bring to America?* If not, then it's probably not the right time for market entry. If yes, then you are ready.

Of course, you can start your US business from scratch without a European parent company. But then, I recommend to self-fund the entire startup process as much as possible—whether through sweat equity or savings.

POTENTIAL STAKEHOLDERS ARE UNAWARE OF YOUR PRODUCT OR SERVICE

If no one's aware of you, then you have to create that awareness. That could mean reaching out to potential business partners or customers here in the US. If you can't drum up interest around your product or service, it is likely that a market entry in and of itself won't generate the interest to sustain your US subsidiary.

As part of your engineered business plan, consider working with a US-based marketer or distributor, attending trade shows, or doing product presentations. There are plenty of professionals who specialize in getting your product in front of potential customers. It will cost you some money, but if the market isn't aware of your company, it's a pretty straightforward need, and you have clear options on how to fulfill that need.

INAPPROPRIATE MARKET

There are several Dutch companies I've been advising that came to the US to present their idea for bicycle-related products and services. With proof of concept, previous success, and all of the other factors that make market entry timing perfect, they chose two target locations: California and Texas.

In this particular case, they got their timing half-right. Don't forget, the US market is actually an amalgamation of many markets (many states with local regulations and economic goals). Right now, California is very welcoming to alternative and eco-friendly forms of transportation, such as bicycles. At the time one of these Dutch companies was ready to enter the market, California was a perfect match. However, Texas' market isn't as ready yet—maybe with the exception of Austin. The biggest continental state is still very much tied to their love of big cars. It's still too early to enter the Texas market with bicycle-related products and services, and some of these Dutch companies didn't engineer their timing strategy in a way that adequately reflected market circumstances.

In order to "fix" the timing in this situation, a company should be proactive about its market analysis. Because, in this example, the Dutch companies were arguably too early, they could also reach out to their team—lawyer, banker, accountant, and insurance broker—to see how they could improve their approach or find a more appropriate market location. Do your research and prepare a US business plan that reflects the various US markets. Figure out where your product or service is needed *right now*.

TOO LATE

With my call to action of entering the US market now, the unfortunate truth is that *now* might already be too late for your company. The following discussion may indicate the ideal timing for market entry has expired.

NUMEROUS ROUNDS OF FUNDING

If you're a privately held and well-established company, this won't apply to you, as you'll hopefully be self-financing your market entry or have business partners assisting.

Startups and smaller companies, on the other hand, can seek capital through multiple rounds of funding. You're too late if you've already been through series A, series B, and series C of funding. Potential US investors will not be interested anymore for several reasons. First, they'll wonder why it has taken your business so long and so much capital to generate what it needs to enter the market. Second, the shares of the company will likely be so diluted—meaning ownership will likely be diluted—

that there'll be too many cooks in the kitchen trying to make decisions.

This is a cautionary tale because the US is the best place in the world to get venture capital and private equity funding, especially for software and tech companies. There just is no better-suited place to raise capital. Don't overstay your welcome by running through too many rounds of funding before you even get here.

ENTERING THE US MARKET WITH A EUROPEAN BUSINESS PLAN

This timing issue is the other side of the Dutch bicycle companies' stories. Part of their misjudged timing was due, in part, to not fully doing their due diligence on the Texas market. They assumed that, because of their superior product used in different locations all over Europe, their European business plan would work anywhere in the US, too. Instead, they needed a US business plan. There is not much need for bicycle products in Texas because there are not many bicycles and corresponding infrastructure, at least not yet. In that sense, they were too early, because eventually bicycles might populate the Texas market, too.

However, I'm also placing this as being in the "too late" category because there's also another lesson at the heart of the story: needing to overhaul a business plan is a time sink you can't afford. If you come into the US without a business plan appropriate to the target market, you run the risk that competitors with the same or similar product will adopt a better business plan to corner the could-have-been-yours market share.

Now, it just so happens that these Dutch companies don't have to currently worry about competitors beating them to the punch, but the point still stands.

PATENT OWNERSHIP

Sitting around with analysis paralysis, as I have seen time and again, could also lead to somebody else beating you to the patent punch.

If you don't file for a patent in America, you could lose the exclusive protection to sell your iteration of your product. You may have a great product in Europe, but without a patent, a competitor may already sell it in the US market. Worse yet, the competitor could already own the patent. If that's the case, I'm sorry. You're probably too late to enter the market unless you can distinguish your product from your competitor's patented version of it.

Now, if you have a EU patent, please be sure to also *timely* apply for a US/North American patent (usually within one year). Your lawyer should be able to help you with this. You don't want to be in the same situation as a German company that contacted me to also patent their product in the US after they secured patent protection in the EU. Unfortunately, they waited too long after they had received their EU patent. Worse yet, their patent lawyer in Germany never informed them about the statutory deadline for North America. But due to the fact that they made some changes to the product since they secured the EU patent, we were still able to secure a US patent for them. But, as you can imagine, this was a more expensive process, which could have easily been prevented.

WAITING FOR A CONTRACT

Here is a situation I've seen multiple times, and it's one that you should avoid. I've had companies—manufacturers and service providers—looking to enter the US market to generate interest from the US, be it from investors or potential customers.

In these situations, it seems like a no-brainer to incorporate the US subsidiary early on as a way to establish a relationship with these US interests and to show a commitment to the US market. But, in some cases, the company will refrain from setting up an American entity *until* the contract is ready for execution or the first orders have already been received. This mistake can cause at least two potential problems. First, you'll have waited too long to get your processes going, running the risk that your US customer may get sick of waiting and use their downtime to find a more suitable solution for their needs. America is a market of instant gratification. Here we don't want to wait months because you haven't built your infrastructure yet.

Second, and perhaps more importantly, signing a contract *before* incorporating the US entity means that your European company needs to sign the agreement, thereby exposing the European entity to all of the potential legal liabilities you could have placed on the US entity. Remember the first of the *Three Pillars of Limiting Liability*?

JUST RIGHT

In each of the above sections, I've offered some general advice, where possible, on how to "fix" your timing if you're too late or too early to enter the US market. Even so, I still want to cover what scenarios or circumstances typically point to the market entry timing as being just right.

ALREADY EXISTING PROOF OF CONCEPT

This is a continuation of the earlier point. There may be outlier companies, but (as mentioned) most cannot simply come to the US without having a proof of concept. Whether you're looking for funding, customers, or business partners, having a proof of concept on your product is a necessary confidence booster to the people you are looking to begin a relationship with.

DEMAND IN EUROPE

In contrast to the earlier point, you may already have a proof of concept—a product or service you are selling in the European market. Beyond simply selling that product, do you have a proven market share there? If you can answer this question in the affirmative, the timing for your US market entry is *now*.

If you've demonstrated success in Europe, your product is likely to be better than anything on the US market currently. Don't be too late by letting another European company with a similar product get here before you.

STAKEHOLDER INTEREST

As you experience success in Europe, you will likely receive interest from various stakeholders representing the US market. Those could include potential customers or investors (or, in some cases, governmental entities or institutions). But it could also be a direct competitor.

For the latter, you may be their target for a joint venture, a merger, or an acquisition. For most conservative European companies, this outlook is daunting. The idea of letting somebody else have a say in the company you worked hard to establish can feel like a slap in the face. Instead, I ask you to take these moments as a compliment. Use them to get into a growth mindset and realize that this is a good indication you are the right company for entry into the US market.

You could entertain these offers and decide that it is in your best interest to enter a joint venture or be acquired. Or you can reject these offers and keep up the good work. Ultimately, the gestures in and of themselves should sway you into thinking that you can and probably will find success upon entry into the US market.

EXISTING CUSTOMERS IN THE US

This one is pretty straightforward. If you already have a US customer base, selling and shipping internationally, then you already have a foot in the US market. That should signal to you that US customers are making a commitment to you. And if your American customers are making a commitment to you, you should also make a commitment to them. Your market entry timing is *now*. Nurture your US business into serving and growing your US customer base.

Maybe that means more boots on the ground, such as salespeople and managers. Maybe that means opening up a manufacturing plant in the US. Maybe both. It will depend entirely on your goals, what you sell, and your business plan. But, for example, eliminating long waits and costs for your customers because of local manufacturing will earn your customers' loyalty—in addition to potential federal, state, and local incentives.

There is a service mindset in America. People want to be taken care of, customer-wise. If you're interested in establishing a long-term relationship with your US customers, the best way to get them to commit to you is to engage them locally.

YOU ARE WELL-FUNDED

Most European companies, especially mid-market companies—the hidden champions—are well-funded. That means they don't have a lot of debt on the balance sheet. Doing well financially, well-funded companies can service debt well. It's a generalization, but an accurate one, to say that there are more highly leveraged companies in the US than in Europe.

In the face of that financial security, you do have to spend money to make money. That means the likelihood of taking on some debt to enter the US market. Conservatively, that might mean a fixed-rate loan or putting some of the company's savings on the line. As we discussed before, you should always have some skin in the game.

Of course, there's always risk involved with any market expansion. The question becomes, how can you mitigate the risk? Your US service providers, such as myself as a lawyer advising companies, have knowledge on how to approach market entry in ways that not only limit risk but also easily manage it when it does arise.

If you want to grow, your money has to work for you. Be ready to set aside a certain amount for the US market expansion. Don't let your war chest sit on the sidelines doing nothing while losing value to inflation. Even putting money into a retirement account, for individuals, is killing earnings due to inflation. So, if you can find ways to create a return from an investment while not overleveraging your company, then you're in the right position for market entry.

EUROPEAN COMPANY IS SELF-SUFFICIENT

Going hand in hand with being a well-funded company is being a self-sufficient one. You are self-sufficient if your company fully funds everything that leads up to your customers making the purchase.

That your company should strive for self-sufficiency is fairly obvious, in a general sense. But this condition becomes even more important for your expansion in the US market because it is a comparably more expensive market. The risk it carries (as well as the reward) is bigger. Most likely, your US company will not achieve self-sufficiency immediately. And you need to rest on the security of your European parent company to carry the load (as far as you want to take it) to float the US setup until it scales to become a cash cow. The general rule of thumb, and something I see over and over again, is three to five years until the US subsidiary reaches self-sufficient profitability.

TIME IS OF THE EMPHASIS

Be aware that timing can play a big role in the engineered setup of your US operations. If you want to be careful in your market entry strategy, then you need to put quite a bit of emphasis on your choices, making sure your situation is one that reflects the "just right" timing conditions rather than being too early or too late.

As you determine your timing—and if you want advice on your timing—the next step to engineering a successful market entry is assembling your team of service providers. It's like those many scenes from the *Avengers* movie franchise: "Avengers, assemble!" Although you may have decided that now is the right time, scaling your expansion takes more than just you. It requires the right team. Putting together the right team is what we'll turn to in the next chapter.

ASSEMBLING
THE TEAM

"Great things in business are never done by one person. They're done by a team of people."

—STEVE JOBS

Being successful—individually or as a company—means being a team player.

The importance of a team has been reiterated over and over by the great business icons. Whether Oprah Winfrey, Steve Jobs, Arianna Huffington, Elon Musk, Sara Blakely, or Jeff Bezos, they all relied on extensive teams of people to build their success. They just so happened to be the face of the operation, but their success was predicated on a group of individuals. They had their lawyers, their CPAs, and their respective teams, in-house or third-party. They needed employees. Nobody can do everything by themselves. As the former UCLA coach John Wooden famously said, "The main ingredient of stardom is the rest of your team."

It would be foolish to think that, as a successful company in Europe, you can come to a new market and do it all by yourself. As you *Engineer* your position for market entry, you want to have your *Core Four* service providers established. They include your lawyer, your CPA, your banker, and your insurance broker.

In my experience, most service providers have been around the block before, and locally speaking, we've all worked together or, at least, know each other. As we say in Texas, this is not our first rodeo. That experience and expertise won't merely give you the comforting thought that your market entry may have a higher chance of success in our hands, it will also give you a statistically higher chance of success.

You can trust your team of professionals as guides to the local market. Not only do we have a fiduciary duty to act in your best interest, we also *want* you to be successful. Your success is our success. We are your partners, in a sense. And if you are doing fine, we'll be doing fine, too.

I come from a background of professional football, so I like to think of professional services teams as analogous to sports teams. Like sports, business is much more successful and fun when it's done in a team environment. And like Mark Cuban said, "Business is the ultimate sport." But we need the entire team. A football team without a goalkeeper would have a hard time winning. So, too, would a company without a lawyer have a hard time mitigating risks through a sound legal strategy.

This analogy is transferable to individual sports as well. Even in individual sports, like golf, you have your caddies, doctors, physiotherapists, and everything else required to keep the athlete's mind and body in the best shape. Your professional services team will do the same for you, in terms of keeping your company running as smoothly, profitably, and safely as possible. As your team grows, everyone will be working toward becoming champions of the US market.

THE MANY BENEFITS OF A TEAM

Two words: value and growth. I went to law school and CPAs sit for their exams specifically because our services provide value to you. Although you spend money on our services, the money saved and earned because of service providers leads to the scaled growth potential. In other words, companies that spend more on excellent advice usually make more.

Sure, anybody with some time and good research skills could probably draft up a contract or non-disclosure agreement. But is an owner or an executive writing up the agreement really the best use of their time? Shouldn't their efforts be elsewhere? Further, what's the quality of their work? Without the legal expertise required to mitigate risk, a legal amateur can run into trouble down the road.

Sure, it's tempting to save a buck here or there. Not hiring a lawyer or CPA is one way to do that. You could use online forms. But after you fill out those forms, do you really feel comfortable with them? And as you can imagine, if the proverbial s*** really hits the fan, that money you saved will pale in comparison to the amount you need to spend to fix the mess.

Relying on a team of service providers is more than just paying a bill. It's an investment into a long-term partnership. You can take full advantage of what we have to offer. Through our training and experience, we know what makes our clients successful (and unsuccessful) and can offer objective guidance to assist you in growing your company efficiently.

WORKING WITH US-BASED EUROPEAN SERVICE PROVIDERS

You can go into any American metropolitan area you are thinking of expanding into and find hundreds of American lawyers, CPAs, or bankers, and they will provide a great service to you, no doubt. But they will never see their work through your eyes—the eyes of a European.

The key aspect to creating a successful team for you is looking at the US market through the lens of European service providers already working in the US. It's not just their place in the team that's important, it's also their experience and background. If your service providers have been there, done that, have a European background, and only focus on advising European companies coming to the US, then their expertise is aligned with your goals.

They will understand where you're coming from and what you're trying to accomplish. They will be able to translate your European business sensibilities into what is most successful in America.

For my European clients, we usually assemble a team of service providers who also exclusively focus on servicing European companies in the US. That way, we can ensure that we all "speak the same language" and support the European company toward success in the US. I know many US professionals who advertise themselves as speaking different European languages. But, as you know, it's one thing to learn a specific language in school and quite another to be a native speaker who was born and raised in Europe. My goal for my clients is always to put together a team of professionals who understand your European business mentality because they also grew up in Europe and ideally even speak your language as native speakers.

THE *CORE FOUR*

Teamwork makes the *Modern* American Dream work. Within any team are the central, core players. In the case of business, that translates to a *Core Four*: the lawyer, the CPA, the banker, and the insurance broker. If you hire well in these positions, you'll not only stay out of trouble with your business dealings in America, but you'll also better your chances of flourishing.

Before talking about each core member in more detail, there is one additional guideline for a strong team of service providers. Remember that each of these players has (or should have) an extensive network. Better service providers know (and will have worked with) many other trusted, elite professionals ready to work for you. More so than somebody without any strong European connections.

The order I present the *Core Four* also represents the order in which you should hire, as it is the most business-conducive strategy. For example, hire the CPA before the banker because you will need a US tax identification number (the Employer Identification Number) before setting up your US bank account. Once the bank account is in place, then you can acquire (and pay for) the entity's insurance. All the while, the lawyer can look over your shoulder to make sure everything is being done properly.

THE LAWYER

As we discussed earlier, operating in Europe, your company is usually governed by a civil-law-based system. That kind of system doesn't exist in America. America likes to follow the beat of its own drum. Consider America's use of the imperial system of measurement. The US is aware of the metric system, yet it is sticking with the imperial system. So too is America's judicial system extremely unique.

One major role of your lawyer is to guide you through America's common law system. They should also have at least some expertise in European law. That way, you're getting the best of both worlds and something of a legalese translator. You are used to a certain legal expectation in Europe and probably have very little experience in America. A dual-expert lawyer can help you position your American entity for success while also protecting your assets at home. Ideally, find a US lawyer who is originally from Europe and exclusively works with European companies in the US.

In terms of hands-on work, the lawyer is crucial for setting up the entity structure, filing for entity registrations, and setting up the governing documents. In addition, your lawyer should be able to provide general legal counseling through the backing of a full-service law firm. That way, you only need one contact person (i.e., "your lawyer") no matter what legal support you need: corporate, immigration, employment, litigation, etc. And they can then coordinate behind the scenes within their firm to complete the project. This is also the way I work with my clients.

Think about this fact. Lawyers are often called "counselors," especially in court. This is no accident, as lawyers are your go-to legal counselors. They don't just know the law, they also know what clients can, cannot, should, or should not do. The best lawyers will coach their clients on things not always clear or evident in the law.

Here's a tip: the best lawyers cultivate one-on-one relationships to facilitate the client's needs and get things done—even things that have nothing to do with the law. For example, I always tell my clients I want to be their lawyer for the next twenty or thirty years. That means I usually don't charge them for a two-minute phone call. Your lawyer should also have extensive knowledge of your entity's local area, meaning they should be ready and willing to make hotel recommendations, help you get a tee time at that impossible-to-get-into country club, and just, in general, make things happen for you. As a team member, your professional connection should go beyond the transactional, "Here's a contract to go over."

The biggest mistake you can make with a lawyer is turning away the good ones because they seem too expensive. Let's face the facts: good lawyers in America are expensive (at least as compared to Europe), and nothing is going to change that. They are expensive because of their expertise and because they get results, and in the long run they are making their clients money.

Now, some US lawyers can charge absurd rates as high as $2,000 an hour, so make sure you shop around. If you find a lawyer exclusively focused on representing European clients in the US, you should also be able to expect similar fee structures as in Europe. Also, many such lawyers offer alternative fee arrangements, such as retainer or flat fee agreements. At least that's how I operate.

CERTIFIED PUBLIC ACCOUNTANT

In Europe, it's common to hire a Certified Public Accountant (CPA) and a lawyer from the same firm. That's not allowed in the US. Be prepared that most of your legal and business dealings will require multiple engagements by different firms, perhaps costing more than you are used to. Why is this the case? Generally, it aligns philosophically with America's "checks and balances" system, emphasizing objectivity and multiple perspectives of expertise. If you hired them first, your American-based lawyer should have advised you on this point, but since you're here reading my book, that's a freebie.

With that said, there are many services a quality CPA will provide that are unique. Most obviously, the CPA will handle your tax registrations and returns and keep your tax status active. They will also provide bookkeeping and audit services for your US entity.

If you don't hire a lawyer first, hiring a CPA at the outset is a fine alternative, and your CPA should certainly be able to recommend a lawyer from their network. It is my legal perspective that you should check most elements of your business through your lawyer, but hiring a CPA will grant you access to the next major steps in setting up a US entity.

BANKER

Choosing a banker to suit your needs is critical to avoid slow starts or other mistakes. And it's a little more complicated than walking into a local bank and asking to open up an account, although I've seen that happen plenty of times in my career. That local cashier is, of course, more than happy to open the account. But then a few weeks go by, your internal processing of money begins, and the bank flatly says they can't service your needs because of compliance issues associated with foreign ownership. Then, just like that, the bank account is closed.

You need to approach your banking with care. In my experience, many American banks—especially the big banks—won't let foreign-owned subsidiaries bank with them. But some do. Many bankers have their schtick, or their operational philosophies. Some will only do business with you if you have many millions of dollars in assets. Others won't care about your size, instead evaluating you for risk and growth potential.

Your lawyer or CPA will know the right banks that are willing to work with you. Usually, these banks also don't need you to appear in person to open a US bank account, so that you can handle everything remotely from Europe, if necessary.

INSURANCE BROKER

Arguably, there is a tendency in Europe to over-insure. The US is inverted, as there is somewhat of a tendency to under-insure over here. So, then the question arises: how do you purchase the right amount of insurance coverage to protect both the European parent company and the US subsidiary? As you work with your insurance broker to answer that question, you'll essentially have three options when insuring your US subsidiary: (1) using only your European insurance provider that already insures your European parent company and also offers to insure your US subsidiary under the same policy, (2) using a US insurance company with a separate policy from your European insurer, or (3) a combination of both.

I've represented companies across this range in legal disputes. In my experience, insuring the US subsidiary using *only* the European provider or through the company group insurance policy can lead to bad results, especially in terms of liability coverage. Because of the legal separation the US subsidiary has from the European parent company, it can be difficult to secure sufficient coverage and many exclusions may apply.

When there is a US insurance company providing

coverage to a US subsidiary, it stands a better chance of covering US liability, which only makes sense. Ultimately, this is a better solution, one I've seen time and again prevail.

Ideally, though, the US subsidiary will hold both a US-based insurance policy and additional group or parent-company coverage through a European provider. I call this the "Holy Grail," as it better protects you against potential liability, especially for a lawyer defending your US subsidiary in court.

In any event, ask your US lawyer to check your policies—in particular, any applicable exclusions—before you sign. Unfortunately, I've seen companies that failed to check their policies with their lawyers and missed coverage exclusions that essentially defeated the entire business purpose of purchasing the insurance policy in the first place.

Proper insurance coverage means everyone can sleep better at night. When selecting a US insurance broker, you should pick one who has experience in dealing with subsidiaries of European companies and can also coordinate with your parent company or group insurance carrier.

OTHER SERVICE PROVIDERS TO CONSIDER

There are several service providers to consider that extend beyond the *Core Four*. Your need for the following service providers is dependent upon your circumstances and your company's size.

RECRUITER OR SEARCH CONSULTANT

Essentially, a recruiter or search consultant helps you find your required workforce, whether that be a need for an executive, a general manager, or a janitor. They can also provide market insights into the labor market as a whole, help you review resumes, create compensation and executive compensation structures, coach you on your interview process (what you can ask prospective employees and what you can't), and many other needs. The scope of work they might do for you is wide.

In Europe, working with recruiters or search consultants is becoming increasingly important and more prevalent. Be aware that the day-to-day business in America also relies on the expertise of these individuals. Some placement firms even specialize in recruitment for European companies in the US. Check with your *Core Four* on any recommendations.

As you look to connect with these service providers, keep in mind that many recruiters or search consultants don't actually call themselves such. Some common alternatives are placement service providers, executive search agencies, or employment services.

OUTSIDE HR

You won't need an in-house HR manager if you have five employees or fewer at your US subsidiary. At the same time, you shouldn't use your European entity to handle HR matters at your American branch because, legally, they are different.

For subsidiaries with low employee counts, hiring an outside HR firm will be much cheaper for you when employment issues come up because your next best alternative is calling your lawyer. As your US business grows to, let's say, around thirty or fifty employees, then you should consider hiring an HR manager internally.

BOOKKEEPER

Like an HR manager, many new entities are too small to necessitate their own internal bookkeeper. Until you have the capacity to hire a full-time employee in this role, it would be advantageous to hire cost-friendly, outside help from a bookkeeping firm.

If you want to keep your team smaller, note that many CPA firms offer business bookkeeping services as well.

A WORD ABOUT PRICING

As mentioned, things are more expensive in America. Full stop. Expect to pay more, but also expect that, if chosen well, they will pay for themselves many times over.

Service providers in America face a lack of understanding by Europeans looking to do business in the United States regarding the higher rates. In one story I'm aware of, a Danish client complained to their service provider about rates by making a comparison to Denmark's service provider rates. The problem, of course, is that different markets are different markets and call for different rates. While it certainly produces a high GDP, Denmark's population at the time of this writing is only 6 Million people. That total represents merely one metropolitan region in the US. With more people demanding services in America, limited service providers charge based on the nature of the market.

While you may be used to one thing in Europe, keep everything in perspective. Texas' geography, for example, is bigger than Germany and Austria combined. The lawyer charging you $250 per hour in Copenhagen without experience in American law and not being able to locally serve your American entity, in the long run, will actually cost your company more money than the American lawyer charging you $600 per hour.

Instead of complaining about pricing in the US, do your best to mitigate your costs while not sacrificing quality of service. Look for service providers who focus exclusively on representing European companies in the US. They will charge reasonable fees comparable with similarly-sized firms in Europe.

Elsewhere, price your costs into your product or service. You shouldn't be charging the same dollar amount for your product in the US as you do in Europe by simply converting your currency to US dollars. Everything is more expensive in America, and your product will be, too, thus offsetting many of the costs it takes to enter and stay in the market. Here's a real-world example. A European company signed a more-than-fifty-page-long contract worth nearly $3 Million without having a lawyer look at it for not wanting the expense. I was shocked. To avoid a catastrophe, all this company needed to do was charge their customer at most a few extra thousand dollars (a drop in the bucket on a multi-million dollar deal) to make sure everything was airtight. Any litigation stemming from such a contract would surely cost far more than an initial, litigation-preventative review. And please remember, under US common law, the freedom of contract is quite different from statutory civil law in most of Europe.

Ultimately, as with everything in life, you get what you pay for. Consider that a service provider working at a lower rate is always going to be looking for the next job to keep their income stream alive. Typically, this leads to less attention to detail on the actual work itself.

When it comes to things being good, cheap, and fast, you can only have two at a time. Sure, your online form LLC agreement may work for you at first, but guess what happens if you need to make changes? Online providers are cheap and fast, but arguably their quality is, let's say, less than others. It'll end up costing you more in the long run than having just hired the right person to begin with, which can be good and fast but not cheap. Also, to the contrary, there is no need to pay $1,000 or more per hour as many large national and international firms in the US charge. Find someone who is interested in a long-term business relationship as your trusted advisor. Avoid lawyers who treat your company like a cash cow. Many of my clients actually left these firms after making such realizations.

Working with an American-based European service provider is helpful in many ways, and one of them is explaining to you the market differences and why higher costs are not as terrible as they seem. Don't be that startup that used a lawyer to get started and then never speaks to them again.

Service providers have one product to sell—their expertise. And the only means to deliver that expertise is through their time. Value the time and attention they give to help you grow your business. Are you just looking for a transaction, or are you looking to collaborate with somebody who is excited about doing business with you for decades?

A DREAM TEAM

Creating long-term business relationships helps create trust, and trust creates success. Your dream team can help you stay out of trouble, and if you assemble the team in the right way, they will understand your business and see you as a partner or team member rather than a customer.

With your team assembled, you are ready to move forward with your first actionable step for US market entry—the entity structure of your American business. That will mean collaborating with your lawyer and your CPA, a topic to be covered in the next chapter.

ENTITY STRUCTURE

"No business can succeed in any great degree without being properly organized."

—JAMES CASH PENNY

It is no secret that lawyers, like myself, are big fans of having things properly organized. And if there is anything you take away from this book, instill in yourself that same passion for organization in your US market entry strategy. No business can really succeed without proper organization and entity structure. Of course, it will cost you more money at startup, but when set up the right way, you won't have to worry much later on. The time spent building a solid foundation will pay for itself tenfold.

Remember the *Three Pillars of Limiting Liability*? When engineered well, these pillars will greatly limit your company's potential liability. The first and in my opinion, most important pillar is *Entities*. After that, don't forget, the second and third pillars are *Contracts* and *Insurance*, respectively. We'll talk about those latter two in future chapters. For now, our focus is on entity structure and its utmost importance in protecting your assets—in particular, the assets of the European parent company.

What makes *Entities* the first pillar? Stated simply, the right entity structure has arguably the largest risk-mitigating effect on your business, and best of all, it is the least expensive. It can be done quickly and efficiently, and it is designed to protect the assets of your European company.

PROTECTING THE PARENT COMPANY, PROTECTING YOURSELF

What exactly is at stake if you don't properly set up your organizational structure? Let's look at two examples to find out.

First, a Danish company had been doing business in the US for quite some time without ever setting up a US subsidiary. They used the Danish entity to sign all contracts for their US business and handled all operations remotely from Denmark. Then, of course, something goes wrong and they end up in a lawsuit, which is when they called me. Unfortunately, they indeed screwed up, and the lawyers on the other side knew there was money to be had because the Danish entity is well-funded and owns valuable assets in Denmark—which can be collected against with a US court judgment. Even worse, although the company procured insurance coverage through their Danish carrier, the carrier (as expected) relied on an exclusion to dodge coverage for the company's US operations. Ultimately, we reached a costly settlement. Guess what they asked me to do as soon as they signed the settlement agreement? Set up a US subsidiary entity.

The second example is about an Austrian company I'm familiar with that decided to expand into the American market. They did the right thing to set up a US subsidiary entity, but unfortunately, there was no clear legal division between their GmbH (Austrian company) and their stateside subsidiary (corporation). For example, when they entered into contracts in America, they used their Austrian GmbH as the contracting party and signatory to all of the documents. Unfortunately, something went wrong, and they were sued. In that case, none of their lawyers were able to convince the judge that any collectible assets in America were disconnected from the Austrian GmbH's assets. The Austrian parent company and the US subsidiary became intertwined without proper separation, and that put *all* of the company's assets at risk—ultimately, they also had to pay up.

Here's the lesson: risk is unavoidable, but you can lessen it significantly. And you can't be afraid of litigation in America if you fail to take the right precautionary steps to protect yourself from potential lawsuits.

A proper entity structure allows you to set up separate companies that usually hold little to no assets. But for any applicable insurance coverage, they are judgment-proof. When there's an accident involving your company's products or your company gets sued by a disgruntled employee, the company's assets will be better protected.

But owner fears still linger. The most common among them is what's known as "piercing the corporate veil"—when a judge pierces through an entity structure and applies liability to the European parent company, or worse, personal liability to the managers, directors, officers, or other corporate executives. Thankfully, I'm here to tell you that piercing the corporate veil in US law is very difficult to begin with (also as compared to Europe). Secondly, it is only likely in situations such as egregious fraud—like a Bernie Madoff white-collar-crime type of situation. If you're trying to do things the right way, and since you're reading this book, I'm confident that you are, egregious fraud is probably not on your to-do list. Outside of these situations, corporate law in the US generally protects against personal liability, and if you wish, directors' and officers' liability insurance provides an additional layer of protection. Welcome to capitalism!

ONE US ENTITY IS BETTER THAN NONE

Even if you have only one US entity, you are already much better off than leading with your European entity when entering the US market. Creating that entity puts space between the European company and the risk of liability. Depending on your particular company's structure and size, multiple entities might be advantageous to reduce liability while also creating tax benefits.

There is an important term you'll want to memorize: *blocker entity*. The general understanding is that a blocker corporation or entity acts as a boundary between investors and investment, between subsidiaries and assets. These entities allow you to convert any gains from an investment into corporate dividends distributed by the blocker entity. They also help non-US investors maintain their tax-exempt status.

Borrowing this term from tax law, I like to characterize these entities as having a firm border between subsidiary and parent entities, thereby *blocking* any potential liability that may arise in the US from reaching the European parent company.

For example, a Danish company I represent had a multi-million dollar business in the US without a US subsidiary for some years until they were introduced to me. Fortunately, nothing happened, and of course, if nothing ever happens, it's all good. But it's risky business, and they got lucky. The company representatives were completely unaware of the risk they exposed themselves to because nobody ever worked with them on proper entity structure. I think it is highly problematic that none of their advisors in Denmark ever raised any concerns to them. But we were able to properly set up their US subsidiary, and once again, everyone (especially the ultimate beneficial owners of the company) is able to sleep better at night.

The more thoughtful the entity structure, the better you protect your company against potential risk. If you are dealing with many kinds of assets—such as manufactured products in addition to real estate and intellectual property—you might decide to reduce risk by housing your business operations, real estate, and intellectual property all in separate entities to also separate different types of risks.

Or, you might have different entities for operations in different US states, which each have their own unique laws and regulations that may affect potential liability. For this reason, you might be surprised to learn that nearly 80 percent of US entities are organized in Delaware, including two-thirds of Fortune 500 companies.[4] That's Delaware's business model, right? I tend to say this strategy makes sense if you contemplate an exit strategy involving an IPO or are looking for outside funding.

But most European businesses are privately owned. And for those companies, there is not that big of a benefit to establishing entities in Delaware. There are plenty of business-friendly states that carry numerous benefits for privately-held companies. The biggest benefit is a legal "home-field advantage." Your address will be in the state you are doing business, making you look more favorable to the local market and legal structure. Furthermore, you can avoid a complicated, albeit cheap, system of setting up address services and mail forwarding from Delaware.

For others, it makes sense to divide almost everything into separate legal entities. For one of my German hospitality clients, it makes sense for them to separate each location as its own legal entity (usually, separate LLCs). If something happens at one—for example, a slip and fall by a customer—the assets of all the other locations are still protected.

---

4   Jeffrey W. Bullock, "2018 Annual Report," Delaware.gov, accessed October 29, 2023. https://corp.delaware.gov/stats/2018-annual-report/.

POSSIBLE ENTITY STRUCTURES

There is no one right way to structure your company, but there is a basic framework from which you can work. It is as follows.

At the top, you'll have the parent European company. Underneath that, and 100 percent owned by the parent company, there will be the US entity.

ENTITY STRUCTURE: BASIC

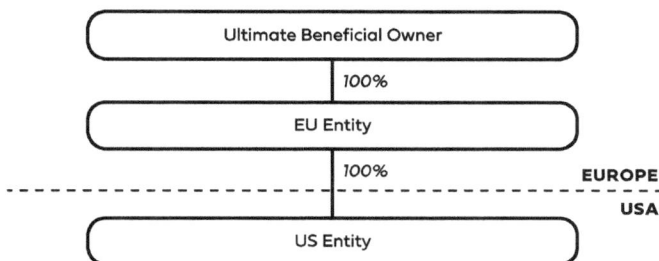

If one subsidiary entity is all you have, then great. US Courts usually have no direct access to the European entity and its assets. Just remember to use your US entity for *all* US contracts and business. Having one US entity is far better risk mitigation than using your European entity for your US business.

For further protection based on your company needs, you can add any number of entities under the US subsidiary's umbrella. That way, you're essentially creating a US holding structure.

ENTITY STRUCTURE: ADVANCED

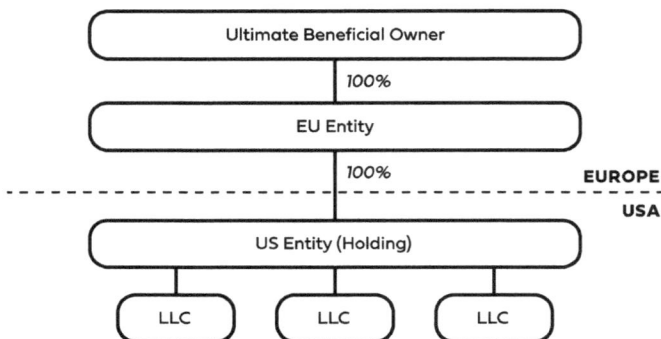

```
┌─────────────────────────────────────────┐
│          Ultimate Beneficial Owner        │
└─────────────────────────────────────────┘
                   │ 100%
┌─────────────────────────────────────────┐
│                 EU Entity                 │
└─────────────────────────────────────────┘
                   │ 100%                        EUROPE
- - - - - - - - - - - - - - - - - - - - - - - -
                                               USA
┌─────────────────────────────────────────┐
│            US Entity (Holding)            │
└─────────────────────────────────────────┘
     │              │              │
  ┌──────┐      ┌──────┐       ┌──────┐
  │ LLC  │      │ LLC  │       │ LLC  │
  └──────┘      └──────┘       └──────┘
```

Perhaps you want one entity, such as an LLC, per location to make sure that an accident at one location doesn't turn into litigation that threatens the assets of another location. Or, maybe the entities represent different products or services your company offers. There are many reasons to create entities, like LLCs, but they are all meant to protect assets by separating them. Hence, the name *limited liability* company.

Keep in mind that both of these examples are fairly basic, straightforward, and for educational purposes only. The entity structure for your company may benefit from more complexity or from country-specific construction. For example, let's consider how a German company might set up its entities. First, here's a visual breakdown of an example of a German entity structure.

ENTITY STRUCTURE: GERMANY

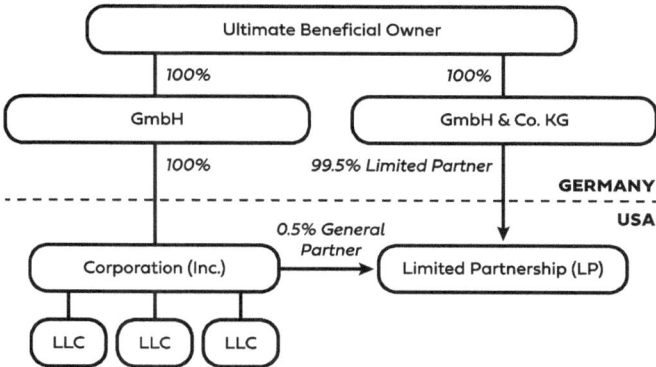

In this country-specific example, the German company is organized as a GmbH—the operating entity—as well as a GmbH & Co. KG for tax advantages for the US operations. For some of my German clients, depending on their circumstances, if they don't already have a GmbH & Co. KG, their CPA sometimes recommends setting one up before market entry in order to take full advantage of potential tax benefits.

The operational GmbH will be the 100 percent owner of the US subsidiary corporation and its LLCs, separate entities which could represent operations in different states, different product lines, or other protective needs for the US and parent companies. Because this structure also requires a limited partnership (LP), we can make the US corporation the general partner of the LP, keeping everything under the umbrella of the parent company's owner. The GmbH & Co. KG holds the remaining 99.5 percent as a limited partner of the LP, and the US corporation only owns 0.5 percent of the US LP, mostly for tax purposes.

Of course, the addition of the holding companies requires more administration—man hours that cost money. However, for many European companies in the US, the cost of administration is far less than the tax savings. When it makes sense, many will opt to have a special entity structure like this to take full advantage of its benefits.

All three structures are great starting points or suggestions. They can get the conversation going with your *Core Four* about where you can add the nuances, if needed.

You may have noticed that I was throwing around terms like corporation, LLC, and LP. For posterity, let's familiarize ourselves with the basic entity types.

TYPES OF ENTITIES

The types of entities that make up your company's structure depend entirely on the European entity's setup and which European country it hails from. In my experience, most European laws tend to favor entering the US market as a corporation. For Germans, the choice is dependent on the parent company's entity structure.

In most cases, US entities can be converted from one type to another if you change your preferences later. Just like you can convert it from one state's laws to another one's. On this note, please keep in mind that you don't establish your entity *in* a specific US state. You establish the entity *under the laws of* a certain state. For example, if you choose Delaware, you really establish the entity under the laws of the State of Delaware. The main office of your US operations is not necessarily in Delaware.

Let's quickly go over various entity types and how they may benefit your overall business structure.

CORPORATION

A corporation (Inc. or Corp.) is a business legal entity governed by statute and is subject to yearly tax filings. Another defining feature is that it is owned by shareholders. The corporation distributes earnings through already-taxed dividends. If your European company is privately held, don't panic quite yet. Corporation "shareholders" can be limited to the private owners of the European parent company. Think of it as a change in title.

Corporations benefit those who have many investors, want to compensate officers with shares of stock, or want a board to oversee and approve officer actions. If you want to be more hands-off, this system puts in checks and balances for you. If your company produces one manufactured product and sells directly to a known customer, then you'll probably be fine with one corporation.

One minor drawback is that the fees associated with creating a corporation compared to other entities are higher due to the statutes governing the business and the documents necessary to complete the incorporation.

Corporations, just like LLCs, enjoy limited liability as long as the shareholders' activities are kept separate from the corporation.

LIMITED PARTNERSHIP

A limited partnership (LP) is when an entity is owned by two or more partners. One partner serves as the "general partner," which oversees and runs the business. The other partner(s) act as the "limited partner," amounting to investors or part-owners. General partners hold unlimited liability for debt, whereas the limited partners are only liable up to the amount of their investment or stake. And there's the tradeoff: general partners run the business but hold the most liability, whereas limited partners aren't in control of the business but have limited liability.

Besides LPs, there are many subtypes of partnerships, such as general partnerships or limited liability partnerships. They all have their advantages and disadvantages, and it's best to seek professional advice on which might best suit your needs. In general, the primary advantage of an LP is limiting liability, especially for the limited partners.

Usually, LPs only come into play if you need a pass-through entity for taxation purposes—like the German example we saw above. When considering the tax benefits of an LP or any other entity, consult your *Core Four*.

LLC

A limited liability company (LLC) is a legal entity governed by a contract between its owners rather than by statute. That provides more flexibility for some, especially smaller businesses. Most of the time, LLCs are taxed on a quarterly and self-reported basis. That means that checks and income won't be taxed, preventing what's called "double taxation" in corporations (taxing both your company's profits and then, separately, your personal income deriving from said profits) and allowing you to reinvest that money immediately in good faith that you'll pay your taxes later. However, an LLC can be taxed like a corporation if you choose to do so.

LLCs are appropriate for businesses that are privately owned or if you prefer tax flexibility. Further, if you plan to have many different localities within the US, you'll want to "wall off" liability as much as possible, making LLCs the natural choice. Another benefit is that decisions won't require complex votes from a board or officers.

"Limited liability" is in this entity's name, so naturally it also enjoys limited liability just like a corporation. Keep in mind that every state has its own LLC asset protection laws. Some states, such as Texas, Wyoming, and Delaware, have aggressive asset protection benefits.

SETTING YOURSELF UP FOR SUCCESS

Many Europeans looking to enter the US market have understandable fears. Potential litigation, excessive liability, and losing everything can't help but infiltrate the minds of many. By and large, though, these fears are misconceptions or downright unfounded.

The solution to these fears has naturally presented itself. Here is your recipe for success: a thoughtfully engineered entity structure. Think of the benefits you'll receive by spending a few thousand dollars to set up your company structure. Absent misconduct, your company's existing assets remain protected, and your future assets have a better chance of protection, which opens the opportunity for scalable growth. You will be able to sleep soundly at night knowing a meager initial investment paid off so well.

Smart companies know that proper entity structure is vital to success. In fact, it is in so much demand, it is the bread and butter of my legal consulting. And it works for companies, as I've seen time and again.

Remember, oftentimes it makes sense to just start with one US entity. More US entities may make sense further down the road, but start with at least one. That simple choice will protect the assets of your European company. If things end up not working out in America, you'll be able to dissolve the US entity and return to Europe without having risked any European assets and operations.

And when you've properly set up your US company, the next step will be to *Execute* your business plan by breathing life into it and filling it with employees. As you probably know already, this itself creates its own set of problems. How will you practically run the US entity? The execution of your market entry is what we'll tackle next.

Welcome to Stage 3: Execute.

» Stage 3 «

Execute

TRANSATLANTIC MANAGEMENT AND HIRING EMPLOYEES

"Every company has two organizational structures: The formal one is written on the charts; the other is the everyday relationship of the men and women in the organization."

—HAROLD S. GENEE

The correct entity structure can set you up for success, but without the right employees running the business, the potential for success will die. In other words, you need a group of people to *Execute*—the third of the *Four Es of Market Entry*—your company's business plan.

In that execution, the relationship between your managers and employees becomes vital. Improper coordination by the European entity in the management of the US entity can lead to disaster. It's not an entity *or* employees that create success. These two aspects of organizational structure have to work together. Otherwise, trouble may be on the horizon.

That was true for a German company I have been representing since early in my career. When opening their US subsidiary, they chose an inexperienced-with-the-US-market German to be the general manager of this new branch. He also had zero experience in hiring and firing people, let alone any knowledge of US employment laws.

Without that transatlantic experience, a risky situation quickly manifested itself. When they decided not to hire a finalist for the sales manager position, the candidate sent an email to the general manager asking why they didn't get the job. In a preservable electronic document, the general manager stated that the person they ended up hiring was more desirable because of their younger age. What happened next? The candidate sued the company alleging discriminatory hiring practices, sapping it of valuable financial resources necessary for growth. I was able to get the company a fair settlement, but, as you can imagine, it was still costly. For many companies, especially in the startup phase, such a litigious blow can put them out of the US market relatively quickly.

In many countries, hiring based on age is a perfectly reasonable thing to do. In the United States, however, age is a protected class (among others).

This brings me to one of the biggest struggles I see with European companies entering the US market: they do things too much the European way. Instead, it should be an interplay, a collaboration, a coordinated effort between the European headquarters and the US subsidiary.

MANAGERS AND MANAGEMENT STRATEGIES

Please don't use a top-down management strategy, clipping the wings of your American branch to prevent it from flying. Instead, keep them at arm's length to allow room for growth. Managing your US subsidiary requires delicate teamwork between the parent company and the US-based venture.

Ultimately, you must have American management in some capacity. I don't have any problem with sending over a European manager of some sort—maybe they are the general manager or president. But you need somebody—a second in command, maybe a vice president or sales manager—to manage and grow the subsidiary from an American perspective. This individual should be an American or, at the very least, somebody with extensive experience in American business operations. The European manager—and I cannot stress this enough—should also have some type of prior exposure to or experience with the US market. That will keep operational goals and philosophies more consistent between subsidiary and parent.

The European manager can oversee the subsidiary and travel back and forth between the subsidiary and parent company to keep the relationship strong, and the American second-in-command can operate locally to serve the American employees and handle day-to-day operations. In many of the successful companies I've been representing,

I've noticed a pattern of periodically sending an American manager to work at the parent company in Europe, keeping a voice for the subsidiary at headquarters. This way, rather than being treated as a stepchild, the subsidiary's growth is a maintained focus for the European headquarters. Again, the goal is an arm's length relationship between Europe and the US, not a top-down approach.

This two-manager coordinated management strategy fosters a transatlantic exchange or a bridge, of sorts. Both groups are represented the right way and feel heard, and the focus can turn toward growth. And it's important to let the American entity grow, if for no other reason than the fact that, quite often, the US subsidiary can earn more money than the European company and other international affiliates due to the US market's mere size and capitalistic system. As my clients know, the US market can outperform the European market very quickly.

Collaborative management strategies provide support for the subsidiary that top-down management styles lack. It builds a transatlantic bridge that, like any thoroughfare, acts as a conduit for economic growth.

I'd like to extrapolate a little more on what I mean by "keep them at arm's length." There's a fine line between requiring approval for everything and the opposite, giving them too much leeway. I've seen some European companies with almost zero oversight over the actions of their subsidiary. As is usually the case, the European parent company would sell products or services to the US branch, then the US entity would sell to its US customers. Sounds simple enough.

In one particular instance, however, what ended up happening to a German client of mine is that the affiliated US entity racked up a debt of more than $10 Million. The US entity simply kept buying products from the German company and sold them to their North American customers, but never paid the German company back. Instead, local US management, without much oversight from the German company, used those funds for their personal gains—almost like a personal piggy bank. The German company had two options. First, they could force the US entity into bankruptcy and cancel the debt. However, that option would mean exiting the market for some time. The second option, and the one we executed, was structuring a takeover so that the US entity essentially went into 100 percent control (with new management and oversight procedures) of the German company. The German company would have to absorb the debt, but at least now there was room for growth, as their main goal was to remain in the US market. The moral of the story may be this: not enough oversight or too much goodwill can be detrimental and quite costly to fix.

Having oversight and control is key, but so is giving the US entity enough freedom to utilize its knowledge of the American market—especially in sales. What that "fine line" is for your company is something you need to explore, possibly with the help of your *Core Four*. It can be as simple as monthly reporting requirements between entities. Regardless, finding the right balance is key. American employees will bring their unique experiences and network to the table, driving the business forward through their knowledge of and experience with the US market.

Market-based realities dictate that your greatest asset is utilizing the expertise of your American employees. Let your service providers and your European manager step in if problems arise.

MANAGERIAL QUICK TAKES

Market Expectations: If you have commission-based salespeople or officers at the US subsidiary, don't be surprised if they start making more money than the executives of the European parent company. The US market can grow quickly, and American salespeople know how to sell. If they are bringing in significant revenue for your company and are contractually rewarded for that, that is only a good thing for your company. Prepare and manage your expectations in this area. Don't put a cap on sales commissions. Otherwise, you are discouraging your American sales employees from performing at their maximum level. Once they reach certain milestones or even their commission caps, they lose their incentive to sell. Even worse, they may leave your company if they receive a better (no-cap) job offer elsewhere.

Two-Way Street: If you are having a hard time giving the US entity its own responsibilities and independence in a collaborative manner, keep in mind that the US managers are not deciding anything for the European company, either. Let the US subsidiary independently decide how to run itself—with coordinated European oversight to achieve the best of both worlds. This is especially true for sales, which is a wholly unique aspect of the American market.

Solicit Feedback: Take responsibility for your screw-ups. Ask your US employees what they are experiencing at the company. Their unique American culture and experience will provide you insight on how to collaborate and why the US managers usually know what they are doing. Talk to your *Core Four*; they can also act as business coaches providing valuable feedback.

EMPLOYEES, HIRING, AND FIRING

European companies can get into trouble easily with employment laws in America. As we discussed earlier, the differences between the civil law system in Europe and the common law system in the United States are vast. Add to those intricacies the slate of protected classes in the US, which mandates that nobody be discriminated against due to their disability, race, national origin, religion, age, sexual orientation, pregnancy, gender identity, or genetic information (such as family medical history). As you know, resumes or CVs in Europe usually include date of birth, a photo, marital status, and sometimes even religious affiliations. If you consider a European-style resume in America, you would run afoul of hiring based on (at least) age, gender, and religion. While it might be perfectly fine elsewhere, asking a question like "Do you plan on becoming pregnant?" is a major no-no in America.

PROTECTED CLASSES

Workers in America have the added protections of legislature and agencies, such as the Americans with Disabilities Act (ADA) and Occupational Health and Safety Administration (OSHA). These additional elements require specific procedures for hiring or maintenance of workspace that ensures you treat all protected classes equally and they enjoy a safe work environment.

Develop a basic understanding of these laws and procedures, whether that's through your lawyer, HR consultant, or recruiter. They are familiar with employment laws and can provide advice on hiring, firing, employment agreements (if you need one), release form language, employee handbooks, and things of this nature. You will need to comply with the laws in these areas because the US is not waiting for you to understand its laws and regulations.

In America, you can sue somebody for almost any reason. Some of my clients are worried about litigation even if they fire an employee without cause (i.e., for no reason). That's why I often advise them to ask the employees who are let go to sign a separation and release agreement saying they won't sue the company. To encourage signing and to make the agreement enforceable, you usually have to offer some kind of severance package.

DO YOU NEED AN EMPLOYEE HANDBOOK?

If there is a clear need to educate your employees on the dos and don'ts of the company as well as general information, it may make sense to create an employee handbook.

This could include information about how the company does business or the benefits provided to the employees such as vacation plans.

An employee handbook doesn't make a lot of sense if you only have one or two US employees. But as your US entity grows, make sure you put all the relevant information for new hires as well as standard employee practices and information in one handbook. You should review your employee handbook every year or so to reflect changes at the company and in the law.

Keep in mind that an employee handbook is not essential to putting your best foot forward when first entering the US market. This is something you can do later in the process.

EMPLOYMENT AT WILL

Many states in America allow employment at will, to some degree, meaning that companies can hire and fire their employees at any time and for any reason (or no reason). It also means the employees can leave whenever they want. Unlike most other places, the United States (and in particular, these right-to-work states) heavily favors employers with these laws. Subject to their at-will-employment, most of the time, American employees only receive an offer letter without a full-blown employment agreement.

My European clients sometimes struggle with this notion because, in Europe, we are used to long notice periods, the concept of loyalty to employees (and employers), expectations of staying in one job for decades, and many other legal and cultural practices that aren't readily present in America. Sometimes, these known differences lead to fears that key employees—managers and officers—might leave the US entity at any time. My advice to alleviate those fears is to consider employment agreements governing the employer/employee relationship for high-level managers and executives. If an employee agrees to it in writing, you can implement non-compete agreements or a company-specific notice period so that your business will not suddenly be without the proper workforce. Nonetheless, if your company begins to lose employees left and right, it's time to look at your transatlantic management and compensation structures. More likely than not, the bridge connecting the European parent company and the US subsidiary needs repair.

But, at the same time, you can also use employment-at-will laws to your advantage. You don't have to give an employee 120 days' notice of their termination and then watch them do nothing for four months while they collect a paycheck. Instead, you can terminate them immediately and hire another employee the same day.

RECRUITING

You should consider working with a recruiter or search consultant to hire employees. I specifically recommend this practice when it comes to hiring your high-level employees (managers and executives). Finding an individual who is fluent in American English, fluent in your country's language, and has decades of experience in both places is extremely difficult. A needle-in-a-haystack situation. That specialized hire may require a recruiter.

If you are unsure how to hire or find a recruiter, contact your lawyer. They should have plenty of recommendations.

Speaking of lawyers, you can also tap the rest of your *Core Four*. If a service provider has European experience, there is a strong chance that they are connected to excellent candidates for any position in your company. They are happy to make introductions.

Here's a small reality check, though. Working with recruiters or even networking through your *Core Four* isn't a guaranteed success. And just like you pay recruiters in Europe, you'll have to pay the US recruiter if they successfully place a candidate with your company.

Another strategy is to utilize university recruiting. Attend career fairs, conduct on-campus interviews, and participate in off-campus recruitment and networking programs.

SALARY EXPECTATIONS

One of the biggest shocks I witness with European clients is the reality check they experience with US base salaries and bonuses. For the most part, they are much higher in America as compared to European markets, especially for managers and sales representatives.

Reasons for the high salaries vary, but the basic idea is that America encourages competitive, market-determined pricing and doesn't want to set prices. Doing so incentivizes growth and stimulates the economy. In addition, unionization and collective bargaining in the US is less prevalent than in Europe. As a thought experiment, think about sales commissions. Most European companies put caps on commissions to "save money" by limiting employee income. America has learned that, in fact, using these caps costs a company money. A sales rep looking to close a $10 Million deal will work far harder in securing the deal if they know that their income will significantly increase via commission for doing so. On the other hand, if their pay doesn't change regardless of the deal getting done or not, then no harm no foul if it falls through. If they are adding substantial value to your company, it makes sense to add value back to them. Having sales reps make large amounts of money can certainly create issues of jealousy or misunderstanding, but those are the US market realities.

THE AMERICAN WORKER

It is critical to understand that although the culture around employment and management is vastly different in the US than what you are used to in Europe, you can (and should) take full advantage of those differences. While at first glance, and as compared to their European counterparts, the American workers might seem disloyal or overpaid, neither is true. Instead, and just like anywhere else, there are strategies you can implement to incentivize hard work.

Apprenticeships, a system you are probably familiar with in Europe, are one excellent way to foster loyalty while improving the quality of work. They can also ensure a years-long commitment to the company. You can also combat less loyalty with higher salaries—the biggest concern of the American worker—and better benefits. In Europe, prospective employees might heavily weigh total vacation days, insurance, or other benefits when making a decision. In America, salary is king. Sure, you can still set your company apart from US competitors by offering better benefit programs. Just understand that US employees generally value higher salaries more.

Other strategies for incentivizing employees include opportunities for advancement or even something as simple as the opportunity to periodically visit or work for the European headquarters. Americans love traveling to Europe, and being sent to Frankfurt, Zurich, or Paris sounds more like a growth opportunity than a work burden. You should also consider implementing an exchange program that goes the other way, sending European employees to America on work visas. From my experience, this further strengthens the relationship between the European parent company and the US subsidiary.

Ultimately, the lesson you need to learn is the following: don't do business in America exactly the same way you do business in Europe. Instead, manage and hire based on tried and true practices that have garnered success in the American market. If you don't, you'll likely have a lot of turnover. Rather than putting your best foot forward, you'll be dealing with time- and resources-consuming headaches.

Once you hire your employees, the next step to *Execute* is to craft deliberate and protective language for the various agreements that will guide your company's relationship with your employees, customers, and business partners.

LIABILITY, PRODUCTS, AND CONTRACTS

"It's the little details that are vital. Little things make the big things happen."

—JOHN WOODEN

There is always one thing at the top of the European business owner's mind: liability. How can we better protect ourselves against potential liability or claims being brought against a product or company? In addition to *Entities* (the *First Pillar of Limiting Liability*), the answer is taking thoughtful care in building the *Second Pillar of Limiting Liability*: *Contracts*, especially those related to your company's product (or service).

When you properly draft your contracts, good results usually follow from bad situations.

In one unfortunate situation, a German company client of mine had to deal with an executive misappropriating a significant amount of money from the company. We terminated her immediately for cause—a provision in the employment contract stipulated the company's right for immediate termination in the case of fraud and self-dealing (among others)—and sought to recover what she stole. We ended up in arbitration, and the good news was that the arbitrator held every provision and detail we had incorporated into her employment agreement fully enforceable. For example, in that agreement, we circumvented the "American Rule" on attorneys' fees and specifically stipulated that should the company prevail in arbitration, it should also recover attorneys' fees. In the end, the arbitrator agreed with us and awarded my client the full amount that covered both the stolen money as well as all attorneys' fees, fees that represented a larger amount than the total the executive stole in the first place. Because my client, together with their legal team, approached contract drafting in the right way, it was a lot easier for my client to win the case and move past the problem.

Surprisingly, not many companies take the appropriate, preventive steps relating to their contracts. I often hear things like, "We already have European terms and conditions, and they're easily translatable to the US." Too many companies think they can simply translate their contracts or product details into English and be set to enter the US market. Nothing is further from the truth. Missing the details necessary to protect your company (and yourself) against liability and to reserve your rights in case of disputes can come back to bite you.

Saving a little money upfront and betting the whole farm because of faulty contracts is a bad idea. Instead, price your service-provider fees to draft and review your contracts into your product or service. Over time, you'll get a good sense of what works, and your need for a lawyer to review contracts will lessen (but will still exist).

Be proactive with contracts to prevent issues from cropping up. If you don't have to put out contractual fires, you can focus on fine-tuning your product, selling, and growing the company.

LIABILITY

Before we get more specific about how to approach products and contracts, I want to talk a little bit about liability. The big question on many minds when planning to enter the US market and reading this book is, *How do I protect my company and myself from potential liability in the US?* When pursuing an answer to that question, European companies don't always look to their products or contracts as a place to limit liability.

Why is that? I've said it before, and I'll say it again, European products are arguably of better quality. With higher-quality products in tow, there is some misguided belief that their quality will, in and of itself, protect the company from litigation. "Other products will fail, not ours," the thinking goes. That opens you up to risk. Unfortunately, in America's legal system, if you don't set up your contracts properly, somebody will find a way to take advantage and potentially win actual, and maybe even consequential and punitive, damages.

Obviously, there is no such thing as a risk-free environment—no matter where you do business. But if you take simple steps to protect your company and yourself, there is absolutely no reason to fear those egregious jury awards sometimes associated with American courts of law. Working with your lawyer will shore up your legal defenses. In terms of your *Core Four*, you should also work with your insurance broker to limit liability.

PRODUCTS

If you are selling a product, you shouldn't do it without properly executed product-specific agreements. Those come in the form of sales agreements or terms and conditions, including disclaimers. Product liability in the US is on the minds of many European companies, and for good reason. You hear of those outrageous jury awards in the tens (or sometimes even hundreds) of millions of dollars because a jury found that some product caused or contributed to an accident. You can prevent (or at the very least, significantly reduce the risk of) that from happening to you and your products. Let's start with terms and conditions.

TERMS AND CONDITIONS

It's not an exaggeration to say that it is *highly recommended* to have your lawyer review the terms and conditions applicable to your products or services, or the agreement you sign with your customers upon sale. This contract will govern your relationship with your customer and (hopefully) protect your company against potential liability—if done right.

Unfortunately, I still run into clients who choose to simply use their European terms and conditions for their US subsidiary.

In one particular case, the European company set up a US subsidiary, but their translated terms and conditions didn't include any waiver of consequential or exemplary damages. Worse yet, they also didn't cap liability. Without proper limitation of liability, the damages customers could sue for might soar significantly higher than the value of the original contract. And lastly, they didn't include an arbitration provision, which meant we ended up in state court.

This case never went to trial because the *Core Four*, myself included, pointed out to our client that doing so would mean opening themselves up to the risk of bankrupting the US subsidiary. We recommended a settlement, which ended up being very expensive—but fortunately, their US insurance covered most of the settlement amount.

This was a business-to-business sale. The American company suing my client, with their American lawyers, was well aware of the gaps in the terms and conditions. That gave them tremendous leverage in settlement negotiations. Thankfully, the company survived, but it was a tough lesson learned. We subsequently changed their terms and conditions and have had no problems since. You should take the preemptive time to make sure your lawyer tightens the agreements related to your company's product or service, like your terms and conditions.

In another example, the US subsidiary of a Danish company had used translated terms and conditions with references to Danish statutes and dispute resolution in Copenhagen before they came to me. It is *highly unlikely* that these provisions would be enforceable in the US for business in the US. We were able to quickly and efficiently update their terms and conditions to make them compliant with (and enforceable in) the US legal environment.

DISCLAIMERS

Beyond the terms and conditions, another crucial document you should provide to your customers—if applicable—is a disclaimer. Without these, customers may make assumptions based on your marketing, messaging, or other company materials that you do not intend. Without disclaimers, you might be held liable.

I'm reminded of the famous 1999 court case featuring Pepsi on the defense. In their 1996 commercial promoting "Pepsi Points," they advertised that if a customer earned seven million points, they could win a Harrier Jet. They provided no disclaimer in their promotional materials that this was only a joke. Also, they told customers that they could buy points at ten cents per point. One quick-thinking individual realized that he could spend $700,000 to earn enough points to be awarded a $36 Million jet. When Pepsi refused to reward him with the jet, he sued. Thankfully for Pepsi, the judge ruled in their favor. But it could have easily gone the other way.

You should also use disclaimers and warning labels to make sure you will not become a potential target for plaintiffs' lawyers looking for vulnerable targets due to missing documentation.

Prevent the headaches before they even happen by including the proper disclaimers in your product offerings where necessary.

CERTIFICATIONS AND LABELS

It is not enough if your product or service has certification from an EU agency or another European entity. That does not necessarily mean it meets the standards required for American certifications or assures the approval of US state or federal agencies.

One of the biggest issues in this area is California Proposition 65 (Cal Prop 65), a relatively stringent law that is more demanding of goods and services than most other jurisdictions and specific to the food and beverage industry in the State of California. If you try to go anywhere you can buy food or beverages in California—McDonald's, Starbucks, Disneyland—there will be signs up at the entrances warning customers about the harmful ingredients within the foods or drinks.

One German company I represent entered the Californian market selling their staple product, a type of pickled vegetable. Their product, which EU agencies found to be perfectly safe, tested slightly above the minimum threshold levels of lead under Cal Prop 65. They hired me and my firm after a California Plaintiffs' law firm notified them of the "problem" and demanded payment of a penalty. As is typical for Cal Prop 65, they were forced to settle with the law firm to prevent further litigation. Had my client been aware of the issue before entering the Californian market, they could have put a warning label on the product to be compliant. Certainly, a warning label is not ideal, but it would have prevented the fine (and lawyers' fees). Over time, the company would then have the ability to change the recipe to meet Cal Prop 65 standards to remove the label.

WARRANTIES

Warranties are common in Europe. An important difference in America is the addition of the qualifier "limited." Limited warranties shrink your overall potential liability. As the seller, you want the warranty as limited as possible and with as many exclusions as possible so that, if something does happen, you will be as protected as you can be—which is all fair game under US law.

If you are a manufacturer, you can add a limited warranty that governs your relationship with your customers. Depending on applicable state law, it could be three months, a year, or whatever you think makes the most sense for your situation or industry standard. My European clients are always surprised when I tell them they generally have this much flexibility on warranty terms.

Limited warranties are fantastic ways to avoid trouble. Most of the time, US customers feel satisfied and taken care of when a warranty is on the table. When the term of the warranty is up and expired, your liability can go down to almost nothing. You may still get sued, but then we have something to point to in court (or ideally, arbitration).

In one instance, one of my German clients manufactured relatively small valves for huge construction projects. More than ten years after the valve installation, the valve broke and allegedly caused significant damage to the refinery. The plant owner sought damages from my client. However, my client's terms and conditions stipulated a twelve-month warranty period, something the owner agreed to in writing. Pointing to that document was where our defense started and the owner's claim ended. Without a *limited* warranty, my client could have been found liable for a bankruptcy-inducing amount of money. Fortunately, my client also had appropriate insurance coverage to add an additional layer of protection had it been necessary.

Again, don't get in the habit of simply copying and pasting your European approach. Whatever your warranties look like back home, your American customers might be fine with less. If that's the case, you don't have to give them something extra that increases your exposure and potential liability.

CONTRACTS

Warren Buffet once said, "It is impossible to unsign a contract, so do all of your thinking before you sign." Despite what you may be used to in Europe, it is extremely difficult and, at times, impossible to undo a contract in the US without significant expense. Best practice is to *always* ask your lawyer to go over a contract before you sign it. There are too many unique-to-America loopholes and pitfalls waiting in the wings to put you at risk.

But why do we even need written contracts? Don't trust that your customers will pay you. Make a contract with your customers. Don't trust that your managers and executives will fulfill their obligations and protect your company. Make an employment agreement with them. If a full-blown employment agreement is unnecessary, consider the protection of a written offer letter. Without anything signed, almost anything goes with not much to fall back on. Remember, in the US, we don't have many codes and statutes. Courts mainly look to the four corners of your contracts.

One German company I represent just assumed their customers would always pay them on time and in full, and they never used written agreements. All they did was send invoices after they fulfilled customer orders. When customers failed to pay them, they just waited in good faith. They sent no demand letters, and otherwise, had no mechanisms for recovering unpaid funds. Then, one customer owed them around $600,000. Because of their complacency, my client stood to lose all of that amount. We still have methods to recover the funds under various common law theories (and fortunately, we did), but it was a hard lesson for them to learn and could have easily been prevented with written agreements.

From a European perspective, civil law codes and statutes generally dictate commerce. There is very little analysis or extra attention involved, and Europeans generally do business under specific restrictions because of the bureaucratic mechanisms. America, on the other hand, is still the Wild West to some extent. Here, contracts aren't even required. And if they are used, contracts have much more flexibility. Just to reiterate, please use written agreements because how you write and structure your contracts will govern your relationship with customers and business partners.

Approaching contracts in the right way can significantly alleviate the fear of potential liability. As I have mentioned before, generally speaking, Europeans make better quality products. If you also protect your company through proper contracts, the US market is your oyster.

Ultimately, if you sell a product or service that itself demands a contract, those contracts should always be subject to limited liability, limited warranties, waivers of consequential and exemplary damages, and other elements previously discussed. Arguably, the most important contract provision for European companies in the US is the dispute resolution provision.

DISPUTE RESOLUTION

In your agreements, I recommend you always include dispute resolution provisions requiring arbitration and waiving jury trials. For US subsidiaries of European companies, arbitration and its neutral third-party decisionmaker is usually preferable to the court system. Even if your principal place of business may be located there, you probably don't want to end up in a rural East Texas court, facing a local judge, litigating against a local Plaintiff, and presenting your case to a local jury. The first thing the other lawyer will most likely do is to paint you as the European bad guy who is coming in and taking away American jobs.

If arbitration isn't an option, do your best to include dispute resolution provisions that favor federal court over state court, as federal courts (unofficially) tend to be a preferred venue for foreign-owned companies over state courts—also in my own professional experience.

Furthermore, if you select arbitration, you can usually choose from a list of proposed arbitrators. This is advantageous in the sense that you can choose somebody you or your lawyers are familiar with and who has experience with cases similar to yours. If you end up in court instead of arbitration, you may draw a judge who may hear a criminal case at 8:00 a.m., an IP case at 9:00 a.m., a payment dispute at 10:00 a.m., and then an employment or other breach of contract dispute at 11:00 a.m. The variety of litigation the judges experience makes things less predictable for you in the sense that they normally don't specialize in one particular type of case.

RELEASES

Releases, sometimes called "hold harmless agreements," are agreements that limit a company's liability from a variety of things, most commonly from product or workplace injuries as well as allegations of discrimination. From an employment perspective, releases are vital. But releases can be tailor-made to fit any of your particular needs.

For example, if you part ways with an employee, and for whatever reason you want the employee to release your company from possible liability against protected class status, you can ask the departing employee to sign a release stating that they will not sue for alleged discrimination because of, let's say, their age. With this document in hand, they can't later come back and file a lawsuit. Well, technically they can still sue your company, but you'll have the documentation needed to prevail. Arguably, I highly doubt they would even find a reputable lawyer to take on the case unless the lawyer thinks there is a valid argument that the release is not enforceable. Another reason why you should ask your lawyer to draft the release—DIY is *not* the name of the game here.

Obviously, the employee is giving away quite a bit of legal opportunity by signing a release, so it's mandatory to incentivize them somehow by offering what we call "consideration." Depending on applicable state law, severance packages or maintaining benefits or health insurance for a set period of time are two creative ways to do this.

"F*** YOU. PAY ME."

Famed tycoon Samuel Goldwyn once said, "A verbal contract isn't worth the paper it's written on." What I've been emphasizing in this entire chapter—and book, really—is to approach your contracts with enough care to protect your company and yourself from as much potential liability as possible.

But even if you properly protect yourself, bad things can happen. For example, customers or business partners might owe your company money. When things can't be resolved, they can devolve into what lawyers romantically call "f*** you, pay me" confrontations. When I represent clients with well-written agreements in payment disputes, I don't really care about the debtor's excuses for nonpayment. We don't care if their dog ate their homework. Remember my former coach's insight about excuses? We simply point to the contract and ask them to pay up. When contracts are written well, you will have maximum leverage when it comes time to arbitrate or go to court. Or, as Charles Stoss put it, "Contract law is essentially a defensive scorched-earth battleground where the constant question is, 'If my business partner was possessed by a brain-eating monster from beyond spacetime tomorrow, what is the worst they could do to me?'"

USE YOUR CONTRACT DOCUMENTS

Whenever possible, you should be the one supplying contracts to your customers and employees, not the other way around. With employees, it's a given; no employee is writing their own contract (at least they shouldn't). But with customers, it gets a little dicey. Sometimes customers want you to agree to their terms and conditions or use their contract documents. As best as you can, always try to hold the pen and use your own contract documents.

Control your own paper trail, and keep your lawyer involved. For your lawyer to have the paper trail of agreements—all written in their preferred form—will pay dividends when it comes to the negotiation and settlement of disputes. Using your own contract documents will also give you a leg up when customers or employees want to negotiate the contracts. Because you and your lawyer are familiar with the form, you'll know where there's acceptable leeway. It lets you dictate things from the outset.

If it ever comes to a point where you are obligated to sign somebody else's contract documents, never just sign it without both having your lawyer review it and entering into negotiations over the language. Contrary to European standards, several rounds of contract negotiations and exchanges of redlines are common—and even expected—in the US.

PROTECT THE EUROPEAN PARENT COMPANY

Because you will be a foreign-owned company doing business in America, you'll occasionally run into an American customer who asks for a parent-company guarantee. One of my Austrian clients was dealing with this early on in their US ventures. They operate in high-value construction projects, and the materials they furnish are quite expensive. If the product failed, offsetting or reimbursing the value of that failure would mean the US entity itself would go belly up. So, their US customer asked that the European parent company guarantee their performance. I can tell you this right now, ideally, you don't want to be in a position where you have to put the European parent company's assets at stake. Don't do it—unless it makes economic sense for a big sale, such as one where the economic benefits significantly outweigh the potential legal risks. We were ultimately able to agree to a limited parent company guarantee for the first project, and then, because my client proved their worth, quickly removed this requirement for the second and all other projects with this customer.

At the heart of all of this—contracts, warranties, products, terms and conditions, and the whole lot—is protection. Keeping your ducks in order will mitigate risk. Much like your entity structure, contracts are designed to protect the European parent company and your US subsidiary from liability. They are the *Second Pillar of Limiting Liability* protecting the structure of your company from potential liability.

Don't be afraid of litigation and potential liability in the US market. Respect them, but don't fear them. There's so much you can do to reduce risk. My hope is that these pages demonstrate to you the many ways you can limit your exposure to liability. *Entities* are the *First* of the *Three Pillars of Limiting Liability*, and now we've covered the *Second: Contracts.*

With the contracts written and executed, let's take a

bird's eye view of where we are at in the market-entry process. We've hired the team, the transatlantic management is in place, and the contracts have been locked in. With everything ready, it's time to sell, thrive, and grow the company! You've given yourself the opportunity to be as successful as you want your company to be. But even so, there are some major differences between selling in Europe versus the US.

SALES, MARKETING, AND YOUR BRAND

"Your brand is the single most important investment you can make in your business."

—STEVE FORBES

This story might sound familiar to you because you or someone you know may have lived it. A European company with arguably the best product in its specific niche enters the US market but struggles with sales. They apply "standard" strategies, such as sending their European or global salespeople to US trade shows. They set up their little booth and show off how great their products are by combining hands-on demonstrations with explanations by experts who know the product inside and out. The booth generates great feedback and a stack of business cards. Yet, the deals are left on the table of the booth, never closing. Closing the deal, it seems, is something completely different.

From a European perspective, it doesn't make sense. Why aren't the sales coming? It's as if there is some sort of invisible roadblock or obstacle keeping the product from breaking through with US customers. What many European companies fail to do in the *execution* stage is utilize a sound branding strategy alongside a careful approach to sales and marketing—one that is specifically tailored to the US.

In all senses of the word, your brand goes to the heart of your business. Whether it's the quality of a product or service, a reputation, an emotional sales pitch, or something else represented in your brand, what can take twenty years to build can collapse in five seconds. That means thinking about developing and protecting your brand should be a top priority for you.

MARKETING AND GENERATING SALES

As stated numerous times throughout this book, you probably have a better product or service than anything that may already be in the US market, but how do you sell it? Having something of quality is meaningless unless you can sell it.

With Americans, two things drive their decision-making: pricing and emotions. Americans do not always buy based on the quality of the product. They don't necessarily want the sharpest knife, they want to know how the sharpest knife will make their life easier at a reasonable price.

The most successful sales tactics in the US revolve around loving your customers instead of your product. It's also still pretty much a "Good Old Boys' Club," proverbially speaking, of networking and relationship building—a "you scratch my back and I'll scratch yours" atmosphere. Americans do business with people they like, know, and trust. That's why relationship building with your US prospects is so much more important than simply offering a great quality product.

LOVING THE PRODUCT VERSUS LOVING THE CUSTOMER

European companies are used to marketing and sales in such a way that demonstrates their enthusiasm, belief, and love for their product. A seasoned European sales rep knows how to explain the functionality and specifications of the company's product precisely and accurately. This is a fine approach, especially in Europe, but it will not get you very far on its own in the US market. Loving the product should be a supplemental tactic when selling in America. I recommend you have your European sales reps assist their American counterparts rather than lead the pitch.

And what is the leading approach that American sales reps take? They love the customer first and last. That means taking meetings at dinner, perhaps a lavish dinner, and paying for the customer's meal. Maybe that's talking business over a round of golf (that is free to the customer). If you're in the South, that could mean a hunting trip.

It's gifting them tickets to the local professional baseball game after you learn that your customer bonds with their children through baseball.

When the customer feels taken care of—when they feel loved—trust in the professional relationship leads to a sale. Because you have the best product in the market, the performance of your product combined with your love for the customer will keep them a customer for life. The one-two-punch of effective sales and marketing is to let the American sales reps tap into their network and love their customers first and then let the European salespeople, who are probably more knowledgeable about the products, swoop in to answer questions and demonstrate products as needed.

My most successful clients let American employees predominantly do the selling in the US. They are the local people with local knowledge and local contacts. They've been cultivating relationships for years and are already tapped into the market. Not utilizing these folks is where a lot of European companies fall short. Fledgling European companies send their global or European salespeople and run into closed doors. Sure, they may still get meeting invitations, but as you know, it's all about closing the deal. As American salespeople often pride themselves on the ABCs of successful sales: Always Be Closing! In Europe, we usually approach sales differently. I recommend you find local US salespeople for your US subsidiary to tap into their local network for successful US sales strategies.

SPEND MONEY ON SALES AND MARKETING

The US market is a pay-to-play market. On the surface, there is something unsettling about the idea of spending money on lavish dinners, golf rounds, hunting trips, sports tickets, or other amenities to love the customer before making a single sale. That makes sense. But let me tell you a story to explain this strategy's effectiveness.

An Austrian client of mine hired an American sales rep with twenty years of local sales experience, which means twenty years of networking and client retention. When this representative began to sell the Austrian company's product, the rep immediately tapped into their list of contacts. How valuable was this to the Austrian company? Just one of this rep's contacts was looking to order $70 Million worth of product.

The sales rep, having decades of experience with this potential customer, submitted a request for $5,000 to take the prospective buyers to a lavish steak dinner. This sale would have constituted the largest single sale in company history and would have not only met but far exceeded their US revenue goals for the entire year. In the face of that kind of market—one wholly different from the European market they were used to—it would have been foolish to refuse to spend $5,000 to make $70 Million. Paying both to hire an American sales rep and for a lavish dinner was the key to unlocking the door—or perhaps the floodgate—to the US market.

This rep's experience and ability to close deals were so staggering compared to the global sales reps that the Austrian company gave the American rep the title "Business

Development Manager." What is even more important, my Austrian client pays the sales rep handsomely without any commission caps—as they should. So, highly motivated by this first sale, the rep closed two more similarly sized deals within twelve months. What an entry to the US market! As a side note, before signing the contracts and closing the deals, my Austrian client always asked me to review and comment on the draft agreements. Yes, of course, they had to pay for this contract analysis and negotiation. Not only did they price it into their quote, but by doing so, everyone is able to sleep better at night—especially when the project value is $70 Million.

Whatever an exciting order looks like for your company in Europe, larger orders are waiting in the American market. It's on a grander scale over here. Once you become aware of that and use a "love the customer" strategy to properly tap into that market, only the sky's the limit. Invest in your relationships with your customers, and invest in the people (American sales reps) who cultivate your relationships with the customers.

THE NEW "GOOD OLD BOYS' CLUB"

More often than not, European marketing and sales strategies involve asking the customer to have a relationship with the company rather than the sales rep. A German client of mine, for example, does business all over the world. When their sales and marketing reps check in with their Croatian customers, it's one rep this week, another next week, and a third the week thereafter. The customers are tapped into the company through this method, but they usually don't know the faces they come into contact with.

Americans do not operate this way. They want a relationship with company sales reps. Not only do they want a connection with the brand they are buying, but they also want to feel they have their personal contact at the company working directly for them. They want to work with individuals, not entities. The time and the cost associated with establishing these relationships is an understood and accepted part of doing business. The benefits of trust, of checks and balances (or open communication), and of professional entanglement generate a sense of collaboration rather than transaction. Everyone wants to grow together rather than growing alone.

In this way, I characterize the American market as a "Good Old Boys' Club." I don't mean that literally. Instead, the phrase is meant to emphasize the importance of networking and relationships above all else. The product is secondary to people and trust. Always remember, Americans do business with people they like, know, and trust.

Another aspect of this approach is the instant gratification that is expected in the US market. Let me look at the difference between European and American car dealerships to explain. In Europe, the average dealership has around twenty-five new cars on the lot, and if you want to order the special edition, that will probably take nine months to arrive. In America, there are hundreds of cars right there on the lot. There are two of every color in every class, ranging from the feature-stripped cars to the fully-loaded models. The US customer wants the benefit of picking whichever one they want and driving off with it right then and there, should they so choose. If an American customer has to wait a long time for the product they want, good luck. You'll probably lose that customer. The sales network that keeps people connected, or this modern "Good Old Boys' Club," exists in part to serve the US market's instant gratification needs.

MARKET APPEAL

When you look at marketing materials in Europe, whether that's pamphlets or another medium, it's usually a bunch of engineering facts, certifications, accreditations, and information. In America, marketing appeals to emotions and convenience.

In the US market, the customer is the protagonist of the narrative and the product is the tool by which they have a wonderful adventure. Think of the famous 1984 Apple commercial that painted PC use as propagating some sort of dystopian, cult-like future where regular people have been transformed into thralls. The implication in the ad is that using an Apple Macintosh computer is associated with freedom of choice and expression. Note that the commercial did not emphasize the Apple computer had a larger built-in RAM memory than an IBM. Instead, it conveyed to customers that they would have their desired emotional response by using the product: a newfound sense of freedom.

Your company's marketing for the US needs to emphasize your US customer more than your product. What relationships, emotions, or convenience will your customer experience because of their choosing your product or service? That is what you need to emphasize.

PROTECTING THE BRAND

I don't want you walking away from this chapter thinking that your product or service doesn't matter. It very much does. You made your company great in Europe on the back of your product or service and the reputation it has built. And behind the scenes, you need to make sure you protect your brand emanating from your product or service.

You don't want some random person to own the trademark or web domain of your company, product, or service. When your name and brand are in the hands of others, that means you can't control its reputation. Because of this, among other things, make sure to register your patents or trademarks in the US alongside those you may already hold in the EU.

INTELLECTUAL PROPERTY: TRADEMARKS

In the branding world, trademarks trump all, so it's in your best interests to make sure you own the necessary trademarks for your company. This allows you to control your branding, your story, and your reputation. Additionally, it helps you prevail if branding conflicts arise.

To stick with the concept of web domains, it's not

unusual for my clients that somebody else already owns the URL with the name of their trademarked company or product. When a company reaches out to the individual who owns the URL, there is sometimes an outlandish demand for a million dollars or more to give up the rights to the URL. You essentially have one of two options. First, you could ask your lawyer to send a nasty letter reminding them about the legal consequences of their improper use of your trademark. With this letter, we usually include a monetary offer—a few thousand dollars, let's say—that is less money than what it would cost to legally pursue the dispute. Second, and if the URL owner refuses, you could sue them, drag them into court on a trademark dispute, and likely prevail.

The takeaway is that when you own trademarks, you are in a much better position to prevail in branding conflicts. And when you are trying to protect your brand and reputation, you want to have the best legal argument possible. But remember, it's not enough to own your trademark only in Europe. You also have to register it in the US—a step that should be part of any comprehensive market entry strategy.

INTELLECTUAL PROPERTY: PATENTS

We already touched on patents earlier in the book to show that the US market is an opportunistic one. Like they say about the National Football League (NFL), the US market is a copycat league, so to speak. If somebody finds any kind of success, others are going to come along and try to copy the winning formula. Often that means infringing on your patents.

Unfortunately, many of my clients have direct experience with such disputes. One German company I represent discovered that one of their former employees took confidential information concerning their patented products and brought it to a competitor—the very same company that this ex-employee left to work for. The purpose, I would speculate, was for the competitor to outprice the German company.

At first, my client didn't want to do anything about it due to the costs associated with enforcing patent rights. But their inaction began cutting into overall revenue significantly. And the cost wasn't just the bottom line. The brand took a hit, too, because it was no longer viewed as the best-in-market version. Its reputation slowly transformed into a new narrative: the needlessly expensive European option. That, as you can imagine, costs not only present, but also future, revenue. In the end, my client realized it was in their best interest to sue the competitor for patent infringement.

Because the US market is so aggressive, you are going to have to take a stance and shift your mind into being proactive about protecting your brand. Like the initial entry in the US market, this type of maneuver will cost you money upfront. But you'll be accomplishing multiple things. You'll let the industry know that you are no pushover and will take a stance when challenged. Other competitors will take notice and know not to challenge you again in the future.

In the long run, the cost of taking a stance will be a valuable investment for sustaining future revenue (revenue made possible because your brand and reputation did not take a hit). Many Europeans see these kinds of infringement lawsuits as bad press that could hurt the brand. That's not the case in America. Americans consider companies that protect their brand as clever, upstanding professionals who are expressing their love for their customers by protecting their customers' interests.

For example, a different German company I represent also sued a competitor for patent infringement. We were able to secure a favorable settlement, and the German company's only real investment was time because the settlement also covered their attorneys' fees. Although the settlement amount itself didn't put the competitor out of business, the loss of revenue combined with the competitor's inability to deliver a product similar to my client's put them out of business. Where there were once two major players in that particular industry, there is now only one—my client.

On the one hand, my client protected their brand. But they also grew the brand by becoming *the* big player. That brought a lot of prestige to the brand. Customers wanted to be part of that prestige and have a closer relationship with a big player. That brand-protecting benefit wasn't initially on my client's radar, but now—based on their increased revenue—they are reaping the benefits. In the US, it usually pays dividends to stand up for yourself and adapt to the generally more litigation-friendly business environment. If you don't, word travels quickly and you will be taken advantage of—a reputation that may cost you dearly in the end. Just be sure. Similar to trademark enforcement, it's not enough to register your patents only in Europe. You'll also need to register them in the US. Make this part of your overall market entry strategy at the outset.

A COLLABORATIVE APPROACH

The European tactics that have made your company a success in Europe—and possibly in other market expansions—will not necessarily translate to your entry into the US market. It doesn't matter if it's your sales and marketing efforts or your intellectual property. Those things won't ensure success in America. The US is different.

Collaborate with your stateside service providers in protecting your IP. *Execute* this early, as you may find that the legal protections you are seeking are no longer available. If you have to change your product's name, you'll want to do that during the market entry process.

But protecting the brand and writing airtight contracts isn't your only goal here. Use your collaborative, transatlantic management system to train up a primarily American sales crew that emphasizes the customers' needs. As an outsider, you don't necessarily have the means to open the doors to closing deals. That's where relying on the experience and local network of American sales reps will be necessary to both your ability to survive *and* to grow.

GROWTH

"There is no limit but the sky."

—MIGUEL DE CERVANTES

As we wind down the *Third* of the *Four Es of Market Entry—Execute*—the final element to a successful market entry strategy is to have an early eye toward growth. What does that look like?

I have been working with a Danish company that specializes in manufacturing equipment for the fish and shrimp processing industry. Their global revenue is between $5 and $10 Million per year, which is modest even by Danish standards. When they entered the US market in 2022, they took the proper and necessary steps to set themselves up for success and growth. In the first quarter of 2023, their US subsidiary ended up generating more revenue than the parent company had the entire previous year. They made their dream of growth possible by accessing the US market.

The *Modern* American Dream is why you're reading this book. It's why people still come to the US in droves. This market provides a clear opportunity for creating a better life for yourself, your company, and your employees.

If you are a European company looking for growth, this is the market to be in. Of course, this book is not a guaranteed, step-by-step guide to successful market entry. But even implementing only one or two of the strategies outlined in previous chapters will put you on the path to success. And businesses that are properly set up and run tend to experience more success and growth.

The success possible in the US is so much bigger than anything you'll be able to achieve in Europe, simply because this capitalistic market is much more business-friendly. If you have the openness to let success happen, the sky's the limit.

Like my Danish client, you may find yourself in a position where your US entity starts making quite a bit of money. The next questions you need to answer are: How far do you want to take this? Do you want to open up production facilities here in the US? Do you want to expand into different states? Do you want to expand into Canada, Mexico, or another adjacent market now that you're successfully established on the continent? Do you want to acquire a company to expand your offerings? Certainly, growth requires risk, but if you're not growing, you're dying. *Evaluate* and take opportunities that come your way.

BE OPPORTUNISTIC

Be open to growth. Embrace it. Let it happen. Doing so will prevent stagnation, complacency, or the potential death of your company. The European sensibility, most times, is to keep things status quo. That might work in Europe. But in the US, being satisfied with a certain level of success, from a business perspective, usually means stalling until somebody else comes in, does it better, swallows you up, or takes your market share away from you.

Because you are responsible for your company and your employees, it's your duty, to a certain extent, to grow the company. Being on the lookout for growth opportunities is always associated with that duty. And if you are responsible for so much, chances are you are a responsible individual. In other words, you should always look very carefully at business opportunities, doing your due diligence and soliciting feedback and ideas from others within your organization, and from your *Core Four*.

When you have the US entity set up in the right way and approach growth opportunities with due diligence and the support of your *Core Four*, I don't think there is much risk involved at all. Obviously, there is *some* risk, as there always is. But you will have protected yourself against risk in a variety of ways, which results in a better chance of success.

How we understand or define risk in Europe is much different than in the US. In America, companies are much more bullish. It's as if taking chances is part of the standard operating procedure. And since being opportunistic is part and parcel of not only surviving but also thriving, entering the US market with your best foot forward will help you create a playbook for new opportunities that work for you. Sometimes the "best foot forward" means having the ability to potentially cash out and walk away or, better yet, to go public.

CONTEMPLATE AN EXIT STRATEGY

Most US startups have an exit strategy. They plan an Initial Public Offering (IPO) and then possibly cash out by selling their shares. European companies rarely work this way. It's more about generational wealth, sustainability, and succession.

Having an exit strategy and sustained growth seem diametrically opposed at first glance. But keep in mind that your parent company is in Europe, not in the US. That means that if you take a risk and lose, you can always go back home. If you take a calculated risk and sell off, it'll generate a big payday for the parent company that could also mean reentering the US market in the future. Many American companies are looking to get a foothold in Europe, and buying companies with ties to the European market makes any of your US subsidiaries look extremely valuable to them. You stand to make a substantial amount of money even if you angle your growth with a potential exit strategy in mind.

Contemplating an exit strategy should also help you feel more comfortable with embracing bigger opportunities. If you're worried and sitting on your laurels, your exit strategy allows you to take that leap knowing you'll mitigate any ill effects by implementing it. No harm, no foul. When you work with your *Core Four* and put together the parameters of a specific exit strategy, it makes all decisions related to growth a lot easier.

EMBRACE SCALE

Draw up a timeline of achievable growth. This can help you determine many aspects of your business plan such as whether or not the US market is right for your company in the long run, how to make adjustments to the business plan, if or when to implement an exit strategy or any number of things.

In the end, it's a numbers game. Where are you starting? Where do you want to be? And is there a reasonable, evidence-based strategic plan that states the intended growth is achievable? When analyzing the US market, you should quickly see that coming to America can provide sustained growth. In many cases, my clients' US entity easily outperforms the European parent company and other international subsidiaries.

Just consider some of the obvious circumstances. You've achieved success in Europe, a place with (for the most part) a social market economy. What's preventing you from accomplishing more in a capitalistic economy where you have access to fifty states, Canada, and Mexico? Those points alone demonstrate you should be able to scale growth by entering the US market.

Plan for growth, possibly scaled growth. Make goals and projections for the years to come, such as looking to double your US sales figures in three to five years. If you aren't able to achieve that kind of growth and are unhappy with your US subsidiary's performance, rather than dying on the vine, you can always refocus on Europe or other markets.

You may end up selling so much in the US that you feel inclined to tell the US entity to slow down. Clients of mine have panicked about the lack of available raw materials for them to produce and then send their products across the Atlantic Ocean to meet their US customers' needs. To that problem, I simply answer that you are missing an opportunity for scaling growth. Make the investment to open up manufacturing or production facilities here in the US where recent laws have made that a subsidized and tax-advantaged prospect. Increase your production to locally serve the market that wants your products.

FORECASTING GROWTH

Just like the American government has checks and balances, you want to make sure you implement some type of checks-and-balances system for your US subsidiary. Set it up so that it prepares you for growth. You don't simply want to have generic goals of success and market share, you want specific, actionable objectives.

This framework creates the necessary mindset for success. If you're forecasting the potential of your company's future, that requires a hands-on approach from both the American entity as well as the European parent company.

On the one hand, replicating your success in Europe

after entering the US market could theoretically double what you already have. However, and because of what we've already discussed about America being more business-friendly than Europe, you should expect (and forecast) more substantial and possibly scaled growth than what you've seen in Europe.

And the best news of all is that, if you've been heeding the advice of this book, you'll be getting second, third, and fourth opinions from your *Core Four* and other service providers. Even if they ultimately disagree with me, and their assessment is that a forecast suggests temporary stagnation or shrinking of your company, at least you've taken that actionable step for the betterment of your company.

POTENTIAL POWER

"Knowledge is power" is a common adage. My university finance professor added an important and distinct layer to that phrase, saying that he realized early on that education—or the structured acquisition of knowledge—is power. I'd like to add one more layer: *education or knowledge is **potential** power*. Education or knowledge itself does *not* protect intellectual property. Education or knowledge does *not* put together a balanced transatlantic management system. Education or knowledge does *not* write the perfect contract. What does? People taking actionable steps to accomplish their goals. Great planners who don't *Execute* their plans go nowhere. Or, as David Lee Roth put it, "Some people make things happen, some people watch what happens, and some people ask, 'What happened?'" Please don't end up in the second or third category.

Have the education and knowledge, but also have the wherewithal to put that theory into practice.

If you really want to do something, you will find a way while everybody else will find an excuse. If done correctly, it should be so much easier for you to accomplish growth in the US than in Europe. Use the education and knowledge you've gained as *actual* power, not just *potential* power. Don't just put this book away and move on with your life. Take action on what you now know, even if it's a small step. That small step will keep you off the sidelines, transform the stagnation of Europe into growth, and could prevent your company from potentially going out of business.

Reach out to potential service providers. Explore your options. Don't just put away your knowledge.

I put together a checklist with actionable steps for you to take throughout your US market entry journey. You will find the step-by-step checklist at the end of this book. Use it to your advantage and to keep track of your US market entry strategy and, by all means, feel free to adjust it to your specific needs.

But wait, there is more. Who doesn't like a little something extra?

Let's turn to the Bonus Stage: Elevate.

» Bonus Stage «

Elevate

The principal narrative of the book is complete. You've made it! However, there are still many topics relevant to your entry into the US market. The last of the *Four Es of Market Entry* is *Elevate*, and the following chapters will help you do just that. Read on for additional resources, concepts, and market entry options to develop a more complete picture of what will happen if you decide to enter the US market. These bonus materials are meant to *Elevate* the new knowledge you've acquired. In total, the following chapters consider issues that will enhance your overall performance when making that transatlantic transition.

TAXES AND INSURANCE

"In this world, nothing is certain, except death and taxes."

—BENJAMIN FRANKLIN

Before we begin, a disclaimer: as a lawyer, I am not offering professional tax or insurance advice; the information that follows discusses issues that you should bring up to your CPA and insurance broker at your discretion. That's why having your *Core Four* in place and knowing that they regularly collaborate to further your best interest is essential.

When it comes to taxes, there is one major adjustment you'll need to make when transitioning from Europe into the US. Unlike Europe, America separates tax advice and legal advice. Don't forget that you'll need to hire service providers from separate firms. Sure, there are US tax lawyers at US accounting firms. But for a combined US tax *and* legal strategy, you still need to engage two separate firms: one law firm and one accounting firm.

With insurance, which is a completely separate beast, you'll obviously need the counsel of your insurance broker. The reason I grouped taxes and insurance together for this chapter is that, for the most part, the entirety of your *Core Four* will strategize together to get you the best protection in these areas. Often, taxes and insurance will be part of the same, larger strategy.

And while taxes and insurance can be throwaway topics—"We can deal with that later, after we get set up"—the truth of the matter is that well-run companies that maximize their potential for success take a careful look at both during the early stages of market entry.

TAXES

To reiterate, I'm not giving tax advice. What I detail reflects my experience with taxes as it relates to entity structure and startup. And since lawyers should always collaborate with CPAs for entity setup, I will be detailing issues that I've seen. In all situations, contact your CPA for professional tax advice.

TRANSFER PRICING

If you are interested in improving your product or service's pricing, increasing efficiency in your company, simplifying your accounting, or saving on the cost of manpower, then transfer pricing will be a topic for you. Transfer pricing is determining the cost of goods or services that are purchased (or transferred) between related entities or companies.

By fixing the price of transferred goods or services, the goal of transfer pricing is to fix the cost as close to market value as possible. That way, no particular entity receives too much or too little of the associated revenue with the purchase. An even distribution of profits leads to steady profit margins. An uneven distribution of profits could cause one entity to falter.

When it comes to taxes, transfer pricing can reduce the overall tax burden of the European parent company by putting more tax liabilities on the entity with an address in a lower tax jurisdiction. Some companies choose to adjust their pricing if it creates an attractive reduction in the tax burden. The risk, of course, is that this may lock you into selling that same product for less to all other customers lest the IRS take action against your company.

As we already discussed, I see limited partnerships and blocker entities come into play for the most efficient transfer pricing. Talk with your CPA and lawyer together to see if that strategy could also work for your company.

MULTIPLE TAX REGISTRATIONS

The general rule in the US is that your company has to file tax returns in each state where you earn money. That means if you are doing business in all fifty states, you might need to file tax returns in all fifty states. You may find yourself asking questions like, "Do we really need to register for taxes in all states we do business in?" That is when you need to contact a tax advisor to get answers to your questions because the question always is how much nexus (i.e., contact) your company has with specific states—which by its nature, is a factual analysis.

Or consider this. What if you have employees who are working in a different state than the location of the US entity? Generally speaking, the US entity will need to withhold an amount of taxes from the employee's paycheck that represents both where the employee lives and the company (being taxed twice). If the states in question have a reciprocity agreement, then you only need to withhold based on the taxes of the state where the employee lives. Again, for professional advice, these are things to discuss with your CPA or tax lawyer.

Lastly, note that state registrations for tax purposes are different from Secretary of State registrations for legal purposes. Both your lawyer and your CPA will be able to help you keep your company active and compliant with different states' regulations and requirements. And they can also assist you with your mandatory annual reports in the states your company is registered in.

INSURANCE

Insurance is the *Third Pillar of Limiting Liability*, protecting you from liability left unchecked by your entity structure and contracts. Don't let its position in this book fool you. I've sequestered it to the *Bonus Stage* simply because I'm not an insurance broker. Like before, the issues I raise here should not be misconstrued as professional advice. Instead, these are personal experiences from my daily work with insurance brokers that you may find of interest. They are issues that you should consider bringing up with your broker and the rest of your *Core Four*.

When should you acquire insurance on the market-entry timeline? As soon as you've set up your entity, that's when you need insurance coverage. When you sign contracts, you need insurance to ensure you protect your company against potential liability. Many of your US customers will want to see your Certificate of Insurance as part of the contract documents. Some may even require that you list them as additional insureds on your policy.

AMERICAN INSURANCE AGENCIES

There's an insurance mistake we've touched on before, which I strongly suggest you avoid. Many European companies entering the US market assume they can just go to their European insurance provider to insure the US entity via the company group policy as well. Of course, like many places of business, there is a strong chance they will gladly sell you more coverage or additional policies.

Although this is not true in every case, my experience has demonstrated that European insurance companies tend to carry more and tougher exclusions when insuring entities in America. Because each state has its own laws and regulations, the fine print of the lengthy European policy typically carries exclusions that apply only with a deep knowledge of both insurance as well as state and local laws. Of course, you probably will *not* become an expert in applicable state laws. Nine out of ten times, when only using the European insurer, you'll be paying the tab.

What's the best solution? Hire an insurance broker in America who specializes in insuring US subsidiaries of European companies. That will give you an expert who knows both worlds. Then, ask your lawyer to review the policy before signing on the dotted line to make sure your company is, in fact, adequately protected. In one instance, an Austrian client of mine was working with a US insurance broker unfamiliar with representing subsidiaries of European companies in the US and procured a policy that was completely inadequate for their line of business. Fortunately, my client asked us to take a look at the policy before executing it. We were able to point to the shortcomings and then procured a new policy from a different provider that sufficiently protected my client's business.

I compliment clients who want to carry both US and European insurance for their US entity. That's, like I said earlier, the "Holy Grail." But, at the very least, make sure you insure your US entity with a US insurance policy.

If you're curious, and while there are many reasons *why* European insurance companies lean on exclusions, the primary motivating factor is cost. Things cost a lot more in the US. When the European insurance company sees the US claim, it will be much, much higher to pay that out than a similar situation occurring in Europe. Whether that's the lawyers' fees, the legal damages, the repair costs, or anything else. Almost everything is more expensive in the US. As we discussed before, you should expect to pay more for your US service providers as compared to Europe—whether that's your lawyer, CPA, bank account, or insurance coverage. Again, remember the potential upsides of the US market instead of focusing only on costs.

TYPES OF INSURANCE TO CONSIDER

What type of insurance you need will depend entirely on your company, industry, and needs. However, there are some staple insurance policies that will probably apply to your company as well.

Commercial General Liability

As a classic policy, commercial general liability (CGL) protects the insured against claims of property damage, harm from product defect or inadequate service, bodily injury, and personal injury. It usually protects your company against the financial costs that may arise from legal claims based on negligence or accidents.

Most jurisdictions require that larger companies carry CGL. While a legal requirement is one reason to have this insurance, it also provides necessary peace of mind. Furthermore, knowing that your company is properly insured, your customers are more willing to trust your company and opt into the relationship-based sales funnel that dominates American transactions.

Workers' Compensation Insurance

Often shortened to "workers' comp," workers' compensation insurance is necessary if you have employees. It protects employees who suffer work-related issues, such as injuries or illness. The costs covered typically include medical care and wages from missed work.

In most jurisdictions, your company will have to carry workers' comp as a matter of law. But each state has its own rules and regulations for workers' comp. If you believe that workers' comp isn't a necessary part of your company's insurance bundle, such as if you work with independent contractors instead of employees, there are ways to apply for exemptions.

Product Liability

As the name suggests, product liability insurance protects your company against potential liability associated with your product. If your product causes damage to somebody else's property or even worse, causes bodily injury, and that accident is the result of an alleged design defect, manufacturing defect, or an improper warning, you can bet the injured party will likely file a lawsuit.

Like most other kinds of insurance, product liability insurance usually covers medical costs, legal fees, or settlements (within policy limits). Many insurance policies include product liability insurance as part of the commercial general liability coverage, but that's not always the case. If you are carrying commercial general insurance but not product liability (and you sell a product) reach out to your insurance broker to close that gap.

Umbrella Insurance

In essence, umbrella insurance seeks to add coverage where commercial general liability and other insurance policies fall short. For example, CGL usually does not cover libel and defamation. If an employee sues your company for alleged defamation (or damaging their reputation), your CGL policy likely won't cover the legal fees or damages. Or, maybe a guest of yours (not an employee) falls and injures themselves at the location of your US entity. Workers' comp won't cover their medical costs because they are not one of your employees. Umbrella insurance would be required to protect against this potential liability.

The need for umbrella coverage and what might be covered will greatly depend on your company's operations. Explore the niche ways your company may be at risk, and work with your broker to see if umbrella insurance can cover them.

Excess Coverage

Insurance is designed to help us sleep better at night knowing that we have coverage if accidents occur. Even in the face of that, many policies only insure the insured up to a certain threshold—the policy limits. You might still worry about that once-in-a-blue-moon, large accident that could cost your company an amount higher than your policy limits. To solve that problem, consider excess coverage insurance.

This type of insurance protects your company financially at amounts higher than the limit of an underlying liability policy tied to existing coverage. The underlying policy would pay for the claim first until it is exhausted. For anything in excess, the excess liability policy would kick in and begin paying out.

Excess liability is good to have in situations where, after due diligence, you determine that any potential liability your company may face could exceed underlying coverages.

D&O Insurance

Directors and Officers Insurance (D&O) is coverage designed to protect individuals from personal loss arising out of their service as a director or officer of a company. If you are worried about the US court system piercing the corporate veil as part of litigation—which, again, is extremely rare unless there is outrageous conduct involved—consider this policy. Sometimes, I even see directors and officers requesting this insurance coverage as part of their employment agreement negotiations.

If your company is privately held, your coverage only needs to consider the scope and law of state and local jurisdictions. This is because US corporate law is typically handled at the state level. Publicly traded companies are subject to additional federal regulations separate from state and local regulations. In that situation, you can expect slightly more risk, as you'll have a larger body of regulators examining your actions and investigating whether or not to bring suit.

There are three primary forms of D&O insurance, and which form you choose usually depends on your organizational and entity structure.

In the end, as it relates to insurance coverage, remember the "Holy Grail" of coverage we discussed earlier. Ideally, you want to be the company that is covered through its European group or parent company insurance policy *as well as* local insurance coverage via a US policy.

THE US SERVICE PROVIDER
SPECIALIZING IN EUROPEANS

Permit me to reiterate something extremely important. From my experience, you are doing your company a disservice if you select a CPA or insurance broker (or any service provider for that matter) who is unfamiliar with and needs to "learn" the European tax or insurance systems, respectively. Work with somebody who knows both sides of the pond and specializes in both American and European systems—someone who may even be from Europe originally. Without a clear understanding of both systems, a single-system service provider could (unintentionally) get your company into trouble.

The sooner you assemble your team, the sooner you can get a feel for the cost involved with both, and the sooner you can develop a well-informed business strategy going forward. With a sound tax strategy and protective insurance, you will elevate your company's game and position it for sustainable growth.

OTHER MARKET ENTRY STRATEGIES

"There are always alternatives."

—SPOCK

One size does not fit all. This book has outlined a specific (and the most common) type of market entry: opening a US subsidiary. This implies, to some extent, growing organically from one employee. This somewhat conservative approach is attractive to a lot of European companies because, let's face it, most of us are more risk-averse, business-wise. But what I have tried to lay out in this book is also a roadmap to potential success. In fact, nearly 80 percent of my market-entry clients go with the classic route. Still, not all companies coming from Europe want to start from scratch.

Some want to acquire another company right away. Some want to hire the full slate of employees immediately. Some are looking for joint ventures. Or it could be something else entirely. Understand that there are alternatives to the "classic" market entry playbook. In this chapter, I'll briefly discuss other avenues to market entry that might be right for you.

CONSIDERING ALTERNATIVES

Why would you consider an alternative to the "classic" market entry route? Alternative methods to market entry are generally for companies that are more risk-friendly. Taking a riskier approach can elevate and scale revenue quickly. These are companies looking for immediate growth and an immediate, viable platform in the US market. They are very driven, go-getting, and immediate with acquiring their needs. Maybe it's just that they're not patient. Either way, if a company has the means and appetite, choosing an alternative path can cut out some of the more burdensome aspects of the "classic" market entry strategy.

Why do I say that the traditional route can be more burdensome? Let's consider the average American worker. Unlike Europe, there isn't as much worker loyalty in the US, in the sense that it's normal for Americans to frequently change employers. That means attracting, hiring, and training fifty quality employees can take quite a while. On the other hand, you could acquire a company that already has those fifty employees. Perhaps the lump-sum payment for a company, once analyzed, outweighs the time and overall costs of hiring and training from the ground up.

Sometimes the difficulty for market entry stems from working in a niche market. For example, let's say a pharmaceutical products manufacturer is looking to enter the US market. They could take the time to analyze local, state, and federal laws and regulations, hire and train employees, and build FDA-compliant facilities. Or, they could buy an already-established facility to skip the whole rigmarole. This is exactly what one of my German clients did.

These are only a few thought experiments. There could be many reasons that make an alternative route more enticing, not just existing employee or customer acquisition.

ALTERNATIVE MARKET ENTRY STRATEGIES

The biggest obstacle to starting from scratch as a European company in the US is that you don't know what you don't know. That could delay the journey to success. Then, you are not flouting regulations from maliciousness but from ignorance. At that point, the process of market entry would stop, and you would be left trying to get the wheels spinning again.

What follows are some methods by which to avoid the potential miscalculations and blunders that sometimes hold up a traditional market entry.

MERGERS AND ACQUISITIONS

Although "mergers and acquisitions" is the popular verbiage, this term represents many forms of asset consolidations. A merger consists of two or more entities merging to create a new company. An acquisition, on the other hand, is one entity purchasing another. But this term can also refer to consolidations, purchase of assets, an acquisition of management, or tender offers for stock. Most of those are self-explanatory, but I think consolidations deserve to be defined. Consolidations create a new company by combining most of the core businesses of each consolidating entity while tossing and rebuilding the corporate structure.

Mergers or acquisitions can be structured in a variety of ways, including horizontal, vertical, congeneric, and conglomeration structures. Talk to your *Core Four* to discuss the various methods and what might be right for you.

Doing your due diligence for this kind of market entry strategy is vital. If you don't solicit input from your *Core Four* (or wait until after the fact), bad situations can arise. For example, one client of mine brought me their draft contract to purchase a company for $8 Million. My client felt like it was a screaming deal, considering the facility alone, in their estimation, was worth the price tag. They were clearly not risk-averse because their strategy was simply to pray that there was nothing wrong.

Of course, my hope would have been that if they were willing to spend nearly a million dollars, they would have also budgeted some money on due diligence before sending me a contract. I talked them into some targeted due diligence, and the results were not surprising to me. The deal fell through, fortunately for my client, because various factors demonstrated that the purchase price wasn't a viable investment.

As a warning against blind mergers and acquisitions, keep in mind that, although they are not necessarily uncommon in Europe, there are far more liability concerns in the US. Your *Core Four*, with experience on both sides of the pond, will help you navigate those differences.

JOINT VENTURES AND PARTNERSHIPS

Joint ventures and partnerships—or when multiple companies engage in a combined commercial enterprise while maintaining their distinct legal identities—are a delicate market entry strategy to *Execute*. Because there are more parties involved, it can be more difficult to keep everybody happy. For that reason, I usually caution my clients against entering into joint ventures or partnerships at a fifty-fifty split.

It's all about control in a joint venture or partnership. I recommend you only engage in one if you can maintain control, even if it's just a fifty-one to forty-nine split in your company's favor. This is much better because it will give you ultimate decision making power. From my experience, an equal partnership leads to problems.

For anecdotal evidence, one of my clients from Germany entered into a fifty-fifty partnership with a US company. Perhaps logically, because of their local access, the US company was left to run the day-to-day operations. Well, they ran it into the ground. What's worse, the fifty-fifty split combined with a management agreement prevented my client from really being able to do anything about it. Once we had enough leverage to act, my client was able to sue for complete ownership of the company. In the end, they were able to acquire the entity as a wholly-owned subsidiary. But that result came after a years-long headache of a fifty-fifty split that could have been avoided.

You might be thinking something like, *Of course, a US company with no ties to the European company would look to screw them over.* But the truth is that these two companies had a close-knit, trusting, and well-established relationship prior to the partnership. Everything would have pointed to the relationship continuing to be a success. But sometimes bad things happen, and my client did not protect themself against that possibility. They could have saved a staggering amount of money and time had they owned 51 percent instead of 50 percent at the outset.

It can be advantageous to enter into a joint venture or partnership, whether that advantage is putting up less capital, acquiring a management team, or gaining access to needed facilities, materials, or customers. But business divorces do happen. When that day comes and something goes wrong with the partnership, make sure the contracts favor your company and give you control over decision-making. Otherwise, things can get messy very quickly.

WHAT WORKS, WHAT DOESN'T

To even begin considering an alternative market entry strategy, I would advise that you also invest in approaching that alternative strategy the right way. That means due diligence. Have a potential target. Do the analysis on that target. Align its acquisition with your business plan. Use your *Core Four* to research and prepare due diligence reports. Have everyone on the team offer feedback on everyone else's reports. Let management as well as ownership have their say.

Without this front-loaded effort to enter the market with ready-made facilities and employees, the potential downsides far outweigh the upsides—at least in my experience.

RESOURCES

*"Know where to find the information and how to use it—
that's the secret to success."*

—ALBERT EINSTEIN

At this point in the book, you hopefully have a good foundation and a series of major steps from which you can master your company's US market entry. The purpose of this chapter is to provide a list of additional resources and information. These resources may provide additional insights, up-to-date statistics, and market-relevant information. *Elevate* your game by tapping into them.

My hope is that, with these resources, you can find what you need to avoid analysis paralysis. Don't forget that the goal is to take action toward market entry and the growth of your company. Don't use this list of resources as an information-compiling crutch for dilly-dallying.

With each resource below, a current (at the time of publication) website will be provided for your convenience.

AnChams in Europe: Amchams in Europe serves as the umbrella organization for forty-six American Chambers of Commerce (AmChams) in forty-four countries throughout Europe and Eurasia.

Their website is amchamsineurope.com.

CFIUS: CFIUS is an interagency committee authorized to review transactions involving foreign investment in the US as well as certain real estate transactions by foreign persons. They play a role in determining the effects of such transactions on the national security of the US.

Their rather cumbersome website is home.treasury.gov/policy-issues/international/the-committee-on-foreign-investment-in-the-united-states-cfius.

Delegation of the European Union in the US: The Delegation promotes EU policies in the US. This includes, but is not limited to, presenting and explaining EU actions to the US Administration and Congress.

Their website is www.eeas.europa.eu/delegations/united-states-america_en.

Economic Development Organizations: These organizations are dedicated to the economic development of a region, be it a subnational area such as a town, city, county, province, state, a whole nation, or a transnational region unified through economic integration. EDOs are typically government agencies, public-private partnerships, or non-governmental organizations (NGOs) working together with other actors to improve the regional economy they focus on.

One website to locate them is www.trade.gov/selectusa-find-economic-developers.

European American Chamber of Commerce: The EACC provides its members with access to transatlantic business opportunities as well as timely and relevant information, resources, and support on matters affecting business activities between Europe and the US.

For example, one of their websites is www.eacctx.com.

In addition to this resource, you should look at your country's specific Chamber of Commerce. Here is a quick sample (complete with associated websites) of country-specific Chambers of Commerce in the US.

- Advantage Austria, www.advantageaustria.org
- BelCham (Belgian-American Chamber of Commerce), www.belcham.org
- BritishAmerican Business, www.babinc.org
- Danish American Chamber of Commerce, for example: www.daccsw.org
- Denmark in the USA, usa.um.dk/en/about-us/danish-missions/consulate-general-of-denmark-houston/the-trade-department
- French American Chamber of Commerce, national facc.org
- German American Chamber of Commerce, for example: www.gaccsouth.com/en
- Italian Trade Agency, www.ice.it/en
- Italy-America Chamber of Commerce, www.italchamber.org

- Netherlands Business of Support Office, for example: nbso-texas.com
- Norwegian American Chamber of Commerce, www.naccusa.org
- Polish Investment and Trade Agency, www.paih.gov.pl/en
- Swedish-American Chambers of Commerce, www.sacc-usa.org
- Switzerland Global Enterprise, www.s-ge.com/en/sbh

European Commission: The European Commission handles EU trade relations with the US, including the analysis of facts, figures, and latest developments.

Their rather long website is policy.trade.ec.europa.eu/eu-trade-relationships-country-and-region/countries-and-regions/united-states_en.

Internal Revenue Service: The IRS's mission is to provide America's taxpayers top-quality service by helping them understand and meet their tax responsibilities and to enforce the law with integrity and fairness to all.

Their website is www.irs.gov.

International Trade Administration: This is the US resource for competing in the global marketplace. Its mission is to create prosperity by strengthening the international competitiveness of US industry, promoting trade and investment, and ensuring fair trade and compliance with trade laws and agreements.

Their website is www.trade.gov.

Occupational Health and Safety Administration: OSHA's mission is to ensure safe and healthful working conditions for workers by setting and enforcing standards and by providing training, outreach, education, and assistance.

Their website is www.osha.gov.

SelectUSA: SelectUSA is the US government program led by the US Department of Commerce that focuses on facilitating job-creating business investment into the US and raising awareness of the critical role that economic development plays in the US economy.

Their website is www.trade.gov/selectusa-home.

US Census Bureau: The Census Bureau's mission is to serve as the nation's leading provider of quality data about its people and economy.

Their website is www.census.gov.

US Chamber of Commerce: This is the world's largest business organization. Members range from small businesses to chambers of commerce across the US that support their communities. They include the leading industry associations and global corporations that innovate and solve the world's challenges. And they also include the emerging and fast-growing industries that are shaping the future.

Their website is www.uschamber.com.

US Commercial Service: This is the trade promotion arm of the US Department of Commerce's International Trade Administration.

Their convoluted website is www.trade.gov/us-commercial-service#:~:text=The%20U.S.%20Commercial%20Service%20is,exporters%20with%20foreign%20business%20opportunities.

US Customs and Border Protection: Customs and Border Protection prevents people from entering the country illegally or bringing anything harmful or illegal into the US.

Their website is www.cbp.gov.

US Department of Commerce: The Department of Commerce's mission is to create the conditions for economic growth and opportunity for all communities. Through its thirteen bureaus, the Department works to drive US economic competitiveness, strengthen its domestic industry, and spur the growth of quality jobs in all communities across the country.

Their website is www.commerce.gov.

US Department of Homeland Security: DHS is the US federal executive department responsible for public security, roughly comparable to the interior or home ministries in other countries.

Their website is www.dhs.gov.

US Department of Labor: The mission of the DOL is to foster, promote, and develop the welfare of the wage earners, job seekers, and retirees of the US, including the improvement of working conditions, advancing opportunities for profitable employment, and assuring work-related benefits and rights.

Their website is www.dol.gov.

US Equal Employment Opportunity Commission: The EEOC is responsible for enforcing federal laws that make it illegal to discriminate against a job applicant or an employee because of a person's race, color, religion, sex (including pregnancy and related conditions, gender identity, and sexual orientation), national origin, age (forty years old and older), disability, or genetic information.

Their website is www.eeoc.gov.

US Food and Drug Administration: The Food and Drug Administration is responsible for protecting the public health by ensuring the safety, efficacy, and security of human and veterinary drugs, biological products, and medical devices. They also ensure the safety of the food supply, cosmetics, and products that emit radiation.

Their website is www.fda.gov.

US International Trade Commission: This agency of the US federal government advises the legislative and executive branches on matters of trade. It is an independent, bipartisan entity that analyzes trade issues such as tariffs and competitiveness. It also publishes reports on its findings.

Their website is www.usitc.gov.

US Mission to the European Union: The USEU is the direct link between the US Government and the EU.

Their website is useu.usmission.gov.

US Patent and Trademark Office: The USPTO is the federal agency that grants US patents and registered trademarks.

Their website is www.uspto.gov.

US Securities and Exchange Commission: The mission of the SEC is to protect investors by maintaining fair, orderly, and efficient markets. They also facilitate capital formation. The SEC strives to promote a market environment that is trustworthy for the public.

Their website is www.sec.gov.

US Small Business Administration: Created in 1953, the SBA continues to help small business owners and entrepreneurs pursue the *Modern* American Dream. The SBA is the only cabinet-level federal agency fully dedicated to small business and provides counseling, capital, and contracting expertise as the nation's only go-to resource and voice for small business.

Their website is www.sba.gov.

US Social Security Administration: The SSA administers retirement, disability, survivor, and family benefits. It also enrolls individuals in Medicare and provides Social Security Numbers, which are unique identifiers needed to work, handle financial transactions, and determine eligibility for certain government programs and services.

Their website is www.ssa.gov.

USAGov: This entity creates and organizes timely, needed government information and services and makes them accessible anytime and anywhere via the channel of your choice.

Their website is www.usa.gov.

CONCLUSION

"To realize the American Dream, the most important thing to understand is that it belongs to everybody. It's a human dream. If you understand this and work very hard, it is possible."

—CHRISTINA SARALEGUI

The opportunity for a successful market entry into the US is there, and it's ready for you.

It has served so many companies that have come before you. Recall the ones I've used as examples—only a small sample of the European success I've encountered in the US. There's the Danish recycling company that expanded out into Europe and then finally America. Now their American subsidiary outperforms their other branches. Think about the German manufacturer of wind turbine parts and how, with excellent transatlantic management, they trained the employees at their US entity to build and sell well. Or consider the German hospitality company that separated their American locations into separate LLCs all under one holding company acting as the umbrella (and blocker entity) for US operations. Their wherewithal to protect their brand ensured success in multiple jurisdictions. Recall the German manufacturer of valves for construction projects that made sure to include appropriate limited warranties. The protection of their product through contracts mitigated liability for both the US subsidiary and German parent company. Remember the Austrian company that tapped into American sales reps, only to have that choice lead to revenue that far exceeded anything the Austrian parent company could have imagined. And finally, think of the German company which, although initially reluctant, sued a competitor for patent infringement. In protecting itself, it gained a significant market share.

These companies did it the right way and reaped the rewards. They are living the *Modern* American Dream. And that could be your story, too. The *Modern* American Dream is alive, straightforward, and there for the taking.

Now it's up to you to take similar, patient steps in the right direction. Seek growth, but don't be too hesitant. Accept and adapt to the differences in the US market to find success here. However big you want to go and bold you want to be, your goals are possible if you are open to them, listen to your advisors (your *Core Four*), and follow the *Four Es of Market Entry: Evaluate, Engineer, Execute, and Elevate.*

EVALUATE

Europeans looking to enter the US market are often hesitant, and they're wrong for being so. Strip yourself of the myths and misconceptions, reduce your fear, mitigate your risk, and *Evaluate* the real strength of the US market. Right now, there is no other place on the planet welcoming investment and capital like America. Take advantage of that possibility by first resetting your perspective and realizing the current global conditions almost beg for an expansion into the US market.

ENGINEER

Putting your best foot forward isn't just about evaluating the possibilities. You also need to *Engineer* your approach. Take a careful look at how your business would benefit from the best timing. In order to get advice on that and many other aspects of your US market entry, assemble a team of advisors. They will guide you through a successful market entry strategy.

Finally, using your *Core Four*, create an entity and organizational structure that limits potential liability, protects the European parent company, is the most tax efficient, and puts your company in a position to prosper. As the *First Pillar of Limiting Liability*, what you do during entity formation will ripple outward for the rest of the company's existence.

EXECUTE

With the business plan in place, take the leap by *Executing* the plan. Create a collaborative and cohesive transatlantic management system that fosters the delicate teamwork required for the US subsidiary to serve and bolster the European parent company.

Using the *Second Pillar of Limiting Liability*, shore up your contracts, product warranties, employee agreements, and various documents. Tap into the American marketing and sales world. In the American fashion, protect your brand and hire the best employees—and compensate them well.

ELEVATE

With your company on the right track, look for ways to grow. That could include maximizing your tax efficiency, giving yourself room to take risks, or scaling your business through mergers, acquisitions, joint ventures, or partnerships.

Then, rinse and repeat. Utilize your team and the resources around you and start the journey of the *Four Es of Market Entry* over by evaluating, engineering, and executing new opportunities. In the end, the journey will last as long and go as far as you'd like to take it. That's my last piece of advice to you: take the journey.

THE JOURNEY AHEAD

Consider the conclusion of this book as your emergence. You've crossed a threshold and are ready to start your own hero's journey. That fire burning inside you isn't meant to be put out. Stoke it, and take your first actionable steps. Please reach out to let me know how things are going and if there is anything I can do to help. My initial consultations are *always non-binding* and *at no charge*, and I'll be cheering you on along the way.

THE MARKET ENTRY JOURNEY

ELEVATE — Introduction

EVALUATE
- 1. Why You?
- 2. Why the US? Why Now?
- 3. Many Europeans Are Hesitant. Why Are They Wrong?

ENGINEER
- 4. Timing
- 5. Assembling the Team
- 6. Entity Structure

EXECUTE
- 7. Transatlantic Management and Hiring Employees
- 8. Liability, Products, and Contracts
- 9. Sales, Marketing, and Your Brand
- 10. Growth

"THE ROAD NOT TAKEN" BY ROBERT FROST

Two roads diverged in a yellow wood,
And sorry I could not travel both
And be one traveler, long I stood
And looked down one as far as I could
To where it bent in the undergrowth;

Then took the other, as just as fair,
And having perhaps the better claim,
Because it was grassy and wanted wear;
Though as for that the passing there
Had worn them really about the same,

And both that morning equally lay
In leaves no step had trodden black.
Oh, I kept the first for another day!
Yet knowing how way leads on to way,
I doubted if I should ever come back,

I shall be telling this with a sigh
Somewhere ages and ages hence:
Two roads diverged in a wood, and I—
I took the one less traveled by,
And that has made all the difference.

MARKET ENTRY CHECKLIST

This checklist of actionable steps is a step-by-step guide to your company's US market entry. On your own, generate answers to these questions, and check off the list as you answer each item. Use it to your advantage.

This checklist is far-reaching in scope, and each question may not pertain to your situation. Make sure to adjust this checklist to your specific needs.

STAGE 1: EVALUATE

Identify Your Goals—Ask Yourself the Tough Questions!

- What is your current situation?
- What do you want for yourself?
- What is your company's current situation?
- What do you want for your company?

- How can you achieve the goals you have for yourself and your company?
- How can you grow your company's business?
- In which geographic markets do you see sustained growth opportunities?
- What are the pros and cons of the geographic markets you identified?
- What makes the US an attractive market for you and your company?
- What is preventing you from taking the next step toward your goals?
- What is preventing you from entering the US market with your company?

STAGE 2: ENGINEER

Timing—Is Your Company Ready to Enter the US Market?

- Do you have proof of concept that your business can succeed?
- Is there market demand for your business offerings?
- Do you already have existing customers in the US?
  - ○ If so, where in the US are they located?
- Is your business sufficiently funded?
  - ○ If so, how?
- Does the US market know your business offerings?
- Is the specific geographic market in the US ready for your business offerings?
- Do you have a business plan specifically tailored to the US market?

Team—Assemble Your *Core Four*!

- Contact a first potential member of your *Core Four* (lawyer, CPA, banker, insurance broker).
- Remember: make sure they have experience in working with European companies entering the US market (it's a plus if they are originally from Europe).
- Schedule an introductory call, videoconference, or meeting.
- Sign an engagement letter with your lawyer and CPA.

Entity Structure—Make it Real!

- Work with your lawyer and CPA to identify the appropriate entity structure for your US operations.
- Determine under which state's laws you want to form your US business.
- Ask your lawyer to conduct a name availability search.
- Ask your lawyer to form at least one US entity.
- Ask your lawyer or CPA to request the Employer Identification Number.
- Ask your US insurance broker to procure insurance coverage for your US entity/entities.
- Open a US bank account.
- Ask your lawyer to register your entity/entities with the applicable secretaries of state.
- Work with your CPA to register your entity/entities for sales tax purposes.
- Keep your entity/entities active by asking your lawyer and CPA to timely file Annual Reports and tax returns.

STAGE 3: EXECUTE

Employees & Management—It's All About the People!

- Set up bookkeeping systems.
- Ask your lawyer to prepare an employee offer letter or employment agreement.
- Hire your first US-based employee(s).
- Set up payroll systems.
- Set up benefit plans for your employees.
- Ask your lawyer to prepare an employee handbook.
- If applicable, ask your lawyer to apply for US visas/ work permits for foreign employees.

Contracts—Put It in Writing!

- Ask your lawyer to prepare commercial contract templates for your company.
- If applicable, secure certifications for your products.
- If applicable, identify warning labels for your products.
- If you are importing products or components to the US, ask your lawyer to check import regulations.
- Ask your lawyer to review and comment on your written agreements before you sign them (price the review into your business offerings).

Intellectual Property—Protect Your Business and Brand!

- Check your European patent, trademark, and/or copyright registrations.

- Ask your lawyer to conduct an availability search.
- Ask your lawyer to register your patents, trademarks, and/or copyright in North America.

Growth Opportunities—What's Next?

- Together with your *Core Four*, work on a plan to *Evaluate* growth opportunities and scale your business.
- Contemplate an exit strategy.

ACKNOWLEDGMENTS

There are many people who made this book possible, and I would like to thank them for all their assistance, guidance, and help.

First and foremost, thank you very much to my wife, Kim, and our two sons, Conrad and Jacob, for your unconditional love and support. This journey called life would be nothing without you. You have no idea how much I love you!

Thank you to my parents, Sandra and Siegfried, who have always been guiding me, encouraging me, loving me, coaching me, and supporting me. I will forever be grateful for the opportunities you have provided to me! Nothing would have been possible without you and the sacrifices you made. I love you!

Without my late grandparents, Maria and Siegfried, I would have never been able to experience the type of childhood I was blessed with. There is no way to adequately thank them, but I tried to do so when they were alive. I will never forget you!

None of us can have a full and joyful life without friends who bring amusement and richness into our lives. Fortunately, I am lucky to be surrounded by many friends around the world.

To my best friend and brother from another mother, Axel, for always being there for me—on and off the football field—whether in Germany or the US. I know I can always count on you and will always cherish our friendship and adventures.

To my school friends, Tine, Tona, Denise, Steffi, Janina, Dori, Tobi, Timo, Lukas, and Philip, as well as my college friends, Andrew and Konstantin. No matter where we all are, we will always find a way to make time for one another and to celebrate our life accomplishments together. We truly are friends for life!

To my former football coaches at TuS Traunreut, SV Wacker Burghausen, and Saint Leo University for not only teaching football lessons on the field, but true life lessons. Thank you to my former teammates for your camaraderie and the unforgettable memories we made—both in victory and defeat.

To my former professors at Saint Leo University and the University of Houston Law Center for their guidance and education. Thank you for instilling in me the confidence that hard work always pays off, no matter where you are from or which language you speak.

There is no "i" in "Team"—thank you to my current colleagues for their continued support and true team spirit to deliver the best client service imaginable.

To my former colleagues, who took a chance on a

twenty-something-year-old German with a *Far*-East-Texan accent and turned him into a practicing US attorney.

To my business partners all around the world for trusting me with their clients and member companies. Business is a team sport and I am grateful I get to be on your team!

Of course, I want to thank all my clients—some of whom are included in this book—for trusting me with their legal work. Thank you for letting me be your advisor, counselor, and partner in your success. I truly enjoy working with you every single day!

Having an idea and turning it into a book is incredibly difficult, but more rewarding than I could have ever imagined. Thank you to Nick, Maggie, Ryan, John, and Annette for making this a reality. I could not have done it without you!

Last but not least, thank *You* for taking your precious time to read this book and for taking on the journey of entering the US market! I can't wait to see you on the other side.

—Manny Schoenhuber
Houston, Texas, USA—2025

ABOUT THE AUTHOR

Manny is an American attorney, and his mission is to help European companies and investors succeed in the United States.

Born and raised in Germany, he is a lawyer for European investors, companies, and their subsidiaries in the US.

Through his one-stop-shop and client-centric approach to lawyering that builds long-term relationships for growth, his clients experience "the best of both worlds"—a US-educated and Texas-based attorney with European roots. He strives to add value to his European clients' US operations and investments not only by understanding the cultural, societal, and organizational similarities as well as differences between Europe and the United States, but also by guiding his clients through the US legal landscape and all its common-law-peculiarities that are still uncommon to most Europeans.

To date, Manny has supported European companies and investors from over twenty countries.

As a former professional football goalkeeper and collegiate athlete, Manny understands that the strength of the team is the hard work of each individual member. It is his goal to always assemble the right team and to connect his clients with the right business partners for their US ventures.

Manny serves as the Vice Chair of the Board of the European American Chamber of Commerce Texas.

You can reach Manny via email at manny@mastering marketentry.com, or connect with him on LinkedIn here: Manny Schoenhuber | LinkedIn, https://www.linkedin. com/in/mannyschoenhuber/.

Manny's initial consultations are ***always** non-binding* and *at no charge.*

For more information, please visit Manny's website, www.masteringmarketentry.com.

www.ingramcontent.com/pod-product-compliance
Lightning Source LLC
Chambersburg PA
CBHW040851210326
41597CB00029B/4806